MODx 2.0 Web Development

Build dynamic websites with MODx PHP application framework and CMS

Antano Solar John

PUBLISHING

BIRMINGHAM - MUMBAI

MODx 2.0 Web Development

First Edition: March 2009

Second Edition: February 2011

Production Reference: 1160211

Published by Packt Publishing Ltd.
32 Lincoln Road
Olton
Birmingham, B27 6PA, UK.

ISBN 978-1-849513-48-7

www.packtpub.com

Cover Image by Asher Wishkerman (a.wishkerman@mpic.de)

Credits

Author

Antano Solar John

Reviewers

Thayub Hashim Munnavver

Ravishankar Somasundaram

Development Editor

Swapna Verlekar

Technical Editors

Prashant Macha

Manasi Poonthottam

Copy Editor

Leonard D'Silva

Indexer

Tejal Daruwale

Editorial Team Leader

Mithun Sehgal

Project Team Leader

Ashwin Shetty

Project Coordinators

Poorvi Nair

Zainab Bagasrawala

Proofreader

Dirk Manuel

Graphics

Nilesh R Mohite

Production Coordinator

Kruthika Bangera

Cover Work

Kruthika Bangera

About the Author

Antano Solar John is a tech evangelist who is passionate about using technology to revolutionize the learning experience.

Antano has always had the unique ability of learning new technologies quickly when confronted with the challenge of helping experts in that domain. As an accomplished tech-consultant, many organizations turned to Antano when they had tried almost everything and given up. He got involved in training accidentally and has since then trained thousands of programmers.

In the early stages of his career when he was a consultant, he first came across MODx in its infant stages. He mastered it and went on to author the first book to be written on MODx. After which he wrote his next book on a Perl MVC framework called Catalyst.

Eventually Antano was delivering @ Learning, Business and Technology solutions. Later, he joined NuVeda Learning Pvt Ltd as the Chief Technology Officer. Here, he co-authored the patent pending learning methodology titled @ CALF(tm) (Continuous Application of Learner's Feedback)

Antano in his free time focuses on research in Cybernetics and Neuro Linguistic Programming (NLP) as he aspires to build – "School of Excellence" with the vision of Patterning Scalable Methods for Unconscious Excellence.

Antano's first technical publication while in college was "Help AI Help You - Swiss Knife of Communication" in which he attempted to use the machine's intelligence as a feedback device of human communications. Following which he authored "802.11 MAC Enhancements - Breaking Barriers of Wireless Speed" which was published in an IEEE Journal.

Some of Antano's other interests include Music, Dance, Martial Arts and Chess. He used to play Chess professionally as a child-teen. Antano also used to run a successful gaming business when he was in high school through college.

He has also won the yahoo hack award twice, once for developing a Collaborative Browsing Mechanism and consecutively for building a Hybrid Search Engine from scratch.

To those who prepared me,

My Mom & Dad – For all the Hope, Faith, Love, and Wise Counsel.

And to those who made it happen.

About the Reviewers

Thayub Hashim Munnavver has been fascinated by computers and the technologies involved since childhood. He did his tertiary education in Electronics & Communication Engineering at Anna University. Upon graduating, he joined Infosys Technologies Private Limited as a Software Engineer, and worked on the .Net platform, after which he worked as a consultant in Singapore. Currently, he works for NuVeda Learning—a concern that promotes accelerated learning solutions, using technology for people's needs.

> I would like to thank my mother without whom none of this would have been possible, and also Shireen and Vinoshini.

Ravishankar Somasundaram has over five years of experience in providing solutions to clients across multiple sectors and domains. Being more passionate about learning and teaching, he too strongly believes that the sole purpose of learning is to make our minds think in different perspectives, and facilitates the same in his training sessions through a blended learning approach mainly focused on how to "learn to learn".

A Junior Scientist in his lower schoolings, in addition to winning several prizes in science projects, being awarded a prize, by a committee consisting of people from ISRO, the Title in an Inter school Science Fest, for a model display on the "Evolution of Airplanes through Aerodynamics", is one of his childhood achievements.

His final-year college project, which was aimed at eliminating the scenario of English alone being the medium of programming in all programming languages, which restricts people who don't know English from getting into the IT field and implementing their ideas, was selected and funded by MIT NRCFOSS, and is considered a landmark.

Being one of the seven people from India and the only one from Tamilnadu as an official third-party developer of Moodle code, Ravi shares his knowledge by helping people on the Moodle official forum and on its IRC, he has also presented a paper in the 9th International Tamil Internet conference on "Moodle: For Enhanced Learning".

Ravi was a Freelance IT Consultant delivering solutions to firms irrespective of Technical, Non-Technical or Business domains; recently he joined Thirdware Technologies as a Technical Analyst and a Chief Architect heading the R&D Division.

Though I am thankful to all of the people I have met till date, for they contributed to the cause of my growth by becoming an inspiration to me, or by personally guiding and pointing me in the right direction when facing challenging situations or by throwing critiques continuously, making me recognize there is always room for improvement in my career and personal life as well, Meeting a few of these people namely Mr.Madhivanan at my lower schooling as Geography teacher, Mr.Baluchamy at my higher schooling as Physics teacher, Mr.L.Sridhar at SISI as my Hardware and Networking course teacher, Mr.Thiyagarajan and MR.Arul at PAV boxing club as my coaches, Mr.Srinivasan at MIT as Project scientist in NRCFOSS as a guide to my final year B.Tech project, Mr.Antano Solar John at Lynus Academy as my facilitator for perl, Mr.Bala Krishnan at NuVeda as CEO, who completely changed the way I looked at and went about doing things, I am indebted to them.

And, of course, I am thankful to my friends Deepak, Karthik Prabhu, Sesha Gopal, Gopinath, Senthil, Siva, Chandru, Venkat, Naveen, Prem, Sarvothaman, Karthikeyan, Rajesh, Pradeep Kumar, Ranjith Kumar, Rajaram, Mangai, Sridevi , Ramya , Shiva Smruthi and more importantly the IRC community and all the wonderful people dwelling there.

Last but the foremost I dedicate all of my accomplishments to my parents, sister, and other relations, for all the faith, hope, love and support.

www.PacktPub.com

Support files, eBooks, discount offers and more

You might want to visit www.PacktPub.com for support files and downloads related to your book.

Did you know that Packt offers eBook versions of every book published, with PDF and ePub files available? You can upgrade to the eBook version at www.PacktPub.com and as a print book customer, you are entitled to a discount on the eBook copy. Get in touch with us at service@packtpub.com for more details.

At www.PacktPub.com, you can also read a collection of free technical articles, sign up for a range of free newsletters and receive exclusive discounts and offers on Packt books and eBooks.

http://PacktLib.PacktPub.com

Do you need instant solutions to your IT questions? PacktLib is Packt's online digital book library. Here, you can access, read and search across Packt's entire library of books.

Why Subscribe?
- Fully searchable across every book published by Packt
- Copy and paste, print and bookmark content
- On demand and accessible via web browser

Free Access for Packt account holders

If you have an account with Packt at www.PacktPub.com, you can use this to access PacktLib today and view nine entirely free books. Simply use your login credentials for immediate access.

Table of Contents

Preface

MODx is a content management system and PHP web application framework rolled into one. With the ease of a CMS and the extensibility of a framework, MODx allows you to develop professional-looking, intricate websites via its easy-to-use interface and flexible architecture. MODx provides reusable code called snippets, most of which are so generic that, without any modification, they can serve multiple purposes. The generic nature of snippets makes it possible to achieve the perfect customization that is so hard to achieve with other CMSes. This book will have web developers up-and-running with MODx. With the use of step-by-step examples and illustrative screenshots, you will be guided through installation, configuration, and customization of MODx. By the end of the book, you will have created a powerful, dynamic website by using the individual elements of MODx, and without the need for programming know-how.

What this book covers

Chapter 1, What is MODx: In this chapter, you learn the general concepts of web development, and also been assured as to why MODx, as a tool, is a good choice for developing your website. The various development methodologies, especially a CMS and a Web Application Framework are explained. With these briefings on the fundamentals, you will have a clear understanding of what MODx is and why you would want to use it.

Chapter 2, Getting Started: In this chapter, you learn how to set up a working platform for developing websites with MODx that includes the installation and configuration of the prerequisites such as Apache, PHP, and MySQL. To make the process easier, you will use XAMPP, which is a bundle containing all of these packages. Finally, you will install MODx and will verify that everything is set and ready.

Chapter 3, MODx Basics: In this chapter, you learn about resources and containers and how every page that is displayed gets it's content from a resource. You also learn to create, edit, and manipulate resources and manage their configurations, and also receive an explanation of the TinyMCE editor. This chapter also explains each and every configuration option available for documents, and also the general configurable options of the site. Finally, you create a Front Page by using what you have learned, and are introduced to the convenience of the DocManager.

Chapter 4, Templating: In this chapter, you learn about templates, how to create and add them, and the flow of rendering. We learn about template variables and resource specific variables, data types, Widgets, data sources, snippets, and chunks. You also create a template for the site, a snippet from the web, blog functionality, a custom form template for the blog page, and a rich text editor for the blog.

Chapter 5, Authentication and Authorization: In this chapter, you will learn how MODx facilitates authentication and authorization. You will build your site to include user registrations, logins, and user types, and will also set rules on who can do what.

Chapter 6, Content Aggregation: In this chapter, you learn about one very useful snippet, called Ditto. You see how to create aggregation and feeds, and how to create feeds for separate categories. You also learn about tagging and how to tag resources and use them in MODx.

Chapter 7, Creating Lists: In MODx, the simplest way to create lists of all of the resources is by using the `[[wayfinder]]` snippet. In this chapter, you learn how MODx allows us to create these lists dynamically, and you also learn how to present these lists as menus.

Chapter 8, Snippets: In this chapter, you learn how to use the hundreds of snippets that available, and in detail learn how to use a snippet and navigate its custom functionalities. You also learn how to search for snippets that do not come packaged with MODx, and how to use them. Along the way, you will add the functionality required to post comments and to navigate posts via their posting date.

Chapter 9, PHx: In this chapter, you learn how to format the values in template variables, and also see how to make conditional decisions based on the value of template variables, and accordingly present a different output either from the HTML in the expression or from a chunk or snippet.

Chapter 10, Simple Recipes: In this chapter, we will use what we have already learned to study how certain commonly-required functionalities can be implemented. We will learn how to integrate a forum, include an image gallery, and develop forms that can send mail, create web user profiles, and identify similar posts for blogs.

Chapter 11, Creating Snippets: In this chapter, you learn how to create snippets and the different ways of rendering their output. You also learn how to use the available MODx APIs as well as why you should use them. You create a new snippet for the site to display a random fortune. The snippet accepts a parameter for a chunk and renders the output by using chunks and placeholders. You also learn how snippets can make use of external files.

Chapter 12, SEO, Deployment, and Security: In this chapter, you learn how to optimize the site for search engines. You learn about clean URLs, meta tags, site maps, and other tweaks. Having developed the site on a local machine, you learn, in this chapter, how to deploy it to a remote server. Finally, you look into what has to be done in order to make your MODx site secure.

Chapter 13, Plugins and Modules: In this chapter, you learn about plugins and modules. You learn how to use plugins and how to customize plugins. You also learn how to create new plugins, and analyze the code of the prettify code plugin. Finally, you learn how to use modules by using the Autolink module and plugin.

Chapter 14, MODx Revolution: In this chapter, you take a quick look into MODx Revolution, to understand when to upgrade, what to expect, and how to contribute.

What you need for this book

No knowledge of PHP programming or any templating language is needed, but the more advanced chapters towards the end of the book will allow more confident developers to extend their applications even further by creating their own snippets. Software required for this book is only the LAMP Stack and, of course, the MODx installation.

Who this book is for

This book is ideal for newcomers to MODx. Both beginners and experienced web developers will benefit from this comprehensive guide to MODx. The more advanced chapters towards the end of the book will allow more confident developers to extend their applications even further by creating their own snippets.

Conventions

In this book, you will find a number of styles of text that distinguish between different kinds of information. Here are some examples of these styles, and an explanation of their meaning.

Code words in text are shown as follows: "We can set this right by passing the value of the new template variable using the rtcontent parameter."

A block of code is set as follows:

```
<body>
<div id="banner">
<h1>Learning MODx</h1>
</div>
<div id="wrapper">
  <div id="container">
    <div id="content">
      [*pagetitle*]
    <br/>
      [*#content*]
    </div>
  </div>
  <div class="clearing"></div>
</div> <!-- end of wrapper div -->
<div id="footer">It is fun and exciting to build websites with MODx</
div></body>
```

When we wish to draw your attention to a particular part of a code block, the relevant lines or items are set in bold:

```
<div id="wrapper">
  <div id="container">
    <div id="content">
      [*#content*] <!-- This is the only line that is not HTML. It is
explained in the sections below. -->
    </div>
  </div>
<div class="clearing"> </div>
</div> <!-- end of wrapper div -->
```

Any command-line input or output is written as follows:

```
scp index.php username@remotemachineaddress:/foldername
```

New terms and **important words** are shown in bold. Words that you see on the screen, in menus or dialog boxes for example, appear in the text like this: "Click on the **Go** button to import the database."

 Warnings or important notes appear in a box like this.

Tips and tricks appear like this.

Reader feedback

Feedback from our readers is always welcome. Let us know what you think about this book—what you liked or may have disliked. Reader feedback is important for us to develop titles that you really get the most out of.

To send us general feedback, simply send an e-mail to feedback@packtpub.com, and mention the book title via the subject of your message.

If there is a book that you need and would like to see us publish, please send us a note in the **SUGGEST A TITLE** form on www.packtpub.com or e-mail suggest@packtpub.com.

If there is a topic that you have expertise in and you are interested in either writing or contributing to a book, see our author guide on www.packtpub.com/authors.

Customer support

Now that you are the proud owner of a Packt book, we have a number of things to help you to get the most from your purchase.

Downloading the example code for this book

You can download the example code files for all Packt books you have purchased from your account at http://www.PacktPub.com. If you purchased this book elsewhere, you can visit http://www.PacktPub.com/support and register to have the files e-mailed directly to you.

Errata

Although we have taken every care to ensure the accuracy of our content, mistakes do happen. If you find a mistake in one of our books—maybe a mistake in the text or the code—we would be grateful if you would report this to us. By doing so, you can save other readers from frustration and help us improve subsequent versions of this book. If you find any errata, please report them by visiting http://www.packtpub.com/support, selecting your book, clicking on the **errata submission form** link, and entering the details of your errata. Once your errata are verified, your submission will be accepted and the errata will be uploaded on our website, or added to any list of existing errata, under the Errata section of that title. Any existing errata can be viewed by selecting your title from http://www.packtpub.com/support.

Piracy

Piracy of copyright material on the Internet is an ongoing problem across all media. At Packt, we take the protection of our copyright and licenses very seriously. If you come across any illegal copies of our works, in any form, on the Internet, please provide us with the location address or website name immediately so that we can pursue a remedy.

Please contact us at copyright@packtpub.com with a link to the suspected pirated material.

We appreciate your help in protecting our authors, and our ability to bring you valuable content.

Questions

You can contact us at questions@packtpub.com if you are having a problem with any aspect of the book, and we will do our best to address it.

1
What is MODx?

MODx is a content management system and an application framework. MODx makes it quick and simple to create websites that are interactive and that can expose different functionalities, depending on the kind of user visiting the site. The creation of all of this is made possible without the user having any coding background as many of its powerful features work out-of-the-box, without any code changes. MODx and its shipped components are modular and well-abstracted so that the same components provide multiple behaviors, which are determined by how the components are used.

Content management system

A content management system (CMS) allows you to do the following:

- Manage content
- Set content management rules
- Define content

Manage content

Managing content means allowing a user to create, publish, edit, and organize content. A good CMS assumes that the user has no technical knowledge. Hence, it provides an easy-to-comprehend user interface for managing content. A flexible CMS will maintain ease of use, even for a novice, and yet give much flexibility to the professional. Publishing the content must extend beyond just displaying the content, and should include designing how the content is shown, making the content accessible, and allowing easy search of the content, based on various criteria.

Content management rules

Content management rules allow the management of content to be delegated and distributed from just one user to many. Different access levels can be granted to different groups, and users can belong to one or more of the defined groups.

Define content

Managing content is fine, but what exactly is content? A good CMS allows the end user to define what content is. Content can be anything! It can be raw text, pictures, videos, music, or a combination of a few, or all, of them. A necessity in any CMS is to allow the user to define the possible types of content and give such types a name.

An application framework

An application framework is an integrated platform that makes the process of developing and maintaining applications a lot simpler. Often they support a certain development methodology and provide interfaces and tools to make the development rapid and agile.

An application framework serves the following two primary purposes:

- Reusable program components: Any code that has been written once should be available for use within the same application, and in other applications too. This is called reusability. Generally, high reusability is achieved by careful planning and adherence to an objected-oriented paradigm. An application framework reduces the overheads in developing such reusable program components, and handles many of the coding overheads internally.

- Abstracting logic from presentation: In a simpler sense, separating logic from presentation means separating any programming code from the formatting of whatever is finally rendered to the end user (presentation). Ultimately, what a browser can render is generated by the presentation layer and is known as the **Document Object Model (DOM)**. The DOM has a structure, presentation, and behavior. Structure is generally defined by HTML, the presentation by CSS, and behavior by using JavaScript. Separation of logic from presentation means keeping everything that belongs to the DOM away from actual code. Application frameworks help in achieving such a separation by providing what is generally known as *templating languages*. MODx also allows the separation of logic from presentation, but how it helps you to do this is quite different from what is commonly known among developers as templating.

Web development methodologies

The development of websites has evolved over the years. They initially originated from simple hyperlinked pages that provided a wealth of information, evolving to complex objects being exposed as URLs at runtime. When wanting to develop a site, there are multiple options that one may choose for development. A briefing on the most widely known methodologies follows.

Old school—conventional three tiers

The 'old school' approach is to use a programming language to create a complete site or application from scratch without using any third-party templating system or framework. In this method, there are three layers:

- Client-side
- Server-side
- Database access

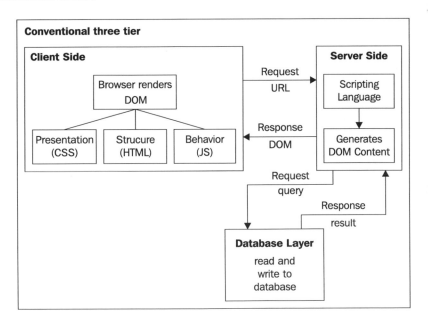

In this architecture, a user requests a page. Every request is processed by executing an appropriate server-side script. A server-side script is any piece of code that is processed and that helps the server to send a response to the client. A common example of a server-side language is PHP. All code that executes in the user's system or the client's system is called **client-side script** or language. HTML and JavaScript are such client-side languages, as they are processed and rendered by the web browser on the user's computer. Whenever needed, any stored information is fetched by the server-side script from the database, and any new information is saved in the database. This approach is called the **Three-Tier Architecture** as, generally, the activities of rendering output, processing the script, and manipulating the database are spread across three layers of systems.

Advantages of the conventional three tiers

One advantage of the conventional three-tier architecture is that it has fewer dependencies. Generally, the only real dependency for such sites is the language itself and the database, if used. Hence, they can be run in any environment that supports the language and, if necessary, the database server. This advantage looks minimal considering the other overheads and the increasing support for CMSs and frameworks among the hosting providers.

The only restriction on what you can do is the limitation of the language itself. Coding everything from scratch, along with the overheads, also brings the flexibility of doing anything exactly the way you want. The only limitation on what can be done and what cannot be done is what is imposed by the language itself. Again, this is not a real advantage as the emerging technologies are being built so abstract that they impose almost no restriction themselves.

The conventional three-tier architecture can be used to develop new development methodologies. Whatever the framework of the CMS may be, beneath the surface, they must all follow the same core rules. Hence, something about these systems takes care of handling requests and generating responses at the lowest layer, which the developer need not worry about. The components that take care of such activities are themselves coded in the conventional three-tier architecture.

Disadvantages of the conventional three tiers

Having to reinvent the wheel is a big disadvantage of the conventional three-tier architecture. Any big project will have a common set of functionalities that are repeated. Many projects have, in fact, emulated an existing CMS or framework in the process of building their own tools. This is just repetition of work and time that could have been spent more productively. Most projects written in the conventional three-tier method end up reinventing the wheel, at least for the concepts of "formatting output" and "database abstraction".

Another disadvantage is that the three-tier architecture is error prone. The language allows you to get things done. It doesn't check if they are done cleanly or not. Hence, it is very simple to write code that gets something done, but not so easy to write clean code that gets the same thing done, even in the worst conditions.

The three-tier architecture is also difficult to maintain. It could be said that code is more read than written. And with this approach, because HTML is mixed with server-side code and appears messy, it is hard to read and maintain such code. Also, if the custom-written libraries are not well documented by the developers who wrote them, then the maintenance becomes even harder as one must read the code to understand its functionalities.

URL mapping becomes complex with the three-tier architecture. It must be noted that in most cases, the job of a server-side script is just to generate client-side output that can be rendered in the browser. So, when such an HTML page with further possible actions is created, the server-side script must be able to generate navigational elements and carefully map the links to a server-side script that can handle the particular request. That is, it has to map a URL to server executable code. This can become tedious to maintain as the site grows, or when a new team is introduced to maintain the code.

Security becomes problematic with the three-tier architecture. The language may have security vulnerabilities, such as SQL injection. Alternatively, there may be security bugs introduced by the programmer. Because, in this approach, all of the functionalities are taken care of by the programmer, there must be strong security testing for all developed functionality and different combinations of use-case scenarios. It is also possible that certain situations can go unforeseen. Writing secure code in such an architecture requires strict discipline, and is laborious.

Templating

Templating is the idea of using files that are very similar to regular HTML files, to render output. These template files have what is known as variable replacement, or commands, similar to a programming language, called directives, that can be inserted within HTML. Hence this approach clearly separates what is called presentation from logic. Apart from this single concept, everything else is the same as the approach mentioned above. Templating also inherits all of the advantages and disadvantages mentioned previously. The ones in addition to those already mentioned are listed below.

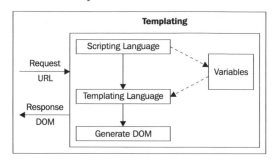

Advantages of templating

One of the main advantages of templating is that view is separated from logic, as explained in the previous figure.

Disadvantages of templating

One of the main disadvantages of templating is that there is a small learning curve for a new templating language. Every new templating language introduces a new syntax and, hence, a small learning curve. The time it takes to learn a templating language depends on the complexity of the system. However, a programmer can generally start using a templating language with just the reference guide or cheat sheets.

Application frameworks

Application frameworks are systems built on top of a programming language to let the developer focus only on the logic of the application. The framework takes care of the other repetitive work. All frameworks at least have the well-known features of "URL Mapping", "DB Abstraction", and "Templating". How each of these is implemented internally is specific to the framework. Every framework also exposes a methodology, the most famous of which is called MVC, which stands for **Model**, **View**, and **Controller**. The framework itself will contain documentations and libraries for frequently used functionalities, thus making the developer's work easier. Every framework also tries to ensure cross-browser compatibility, cross-platform support, and many other clean practices, most importantly the RESTful approach.

For more information on RESTful practices, read www.xfront.com/REST-Web-Services.html.

Advantages of application frameworks

One of the main advantages of application frameworks is that there is a high reusability of code. Frameworks encourage architectures where a higher reusability of code is possible. They also provide enough APIs to do the most common tasks, so that developers don't have to rewrite them.

Application frameworks provide clean practices at no extra effort. Most frameworks follow clean practices, and because they allow you to take care only of the logic, the internals are handled by the framework. Hence, while you may not even know it, you have generated applications that adhere to clean practices!

Application frameworks have good testing mechanisms. Generally, application frameworks also provide some kind of helpful mechanisms to make testing easier. Most MVC frameworks auto-generate test files, or at least generate a very useful skeleton for each unit of functionality being implemented.

In application frameworks, view is separated from logic, which is similar to using a templating language. Most frameworks allow a mechanism for separating view from logic. Some frameworks do this by using a templating language that the framework understands. But this is only one way of doing it, and many frameworks follow different approaches to achieve the same outcome.

Database abstraction means writing a system in such a way that if you were to only change the database server that stores your data, your system would still work without any necessary code changes. Also, most frameworks have an implementation of the concept of **Object-Relational Mapping (ORM)**, which allows the developer to manipulate the database as objects and provide a simple syntax to achieve complex queries.

Disadvantages of application frameworks

When working with application frameworks, there is a big learning curve in understanding the development methodology that the framework understands and expects you to follow. Getting used to a new development methodology can take some time.

All application frameworks have framework-specific syntaxes for a lot of functionalities that they expose. It takes some time to be able to get to the exact documentation when you need it.

Most MVC frameworks have a single templating system, or DB abstraction layer, already defined that you have to use. For some applications, this might be a limitation, or maybe you just prefer something else. This is a small disadvantage. Certain frameworks, like "Catalyst", allow developers to choose individual components as well.

Content management systems

Content management systems are a very interesting idea. The focus of any content management system is that the end user must be able to create websites that can be self-maintained without any programming knowledge. A CMS makes it simple to create the kind of sites that are generally known as **Web 2.0**. Web 2.0 simply means sites in which the content is being displayed is created by the end users and not the developers of the site. There are numerous content management systems, and each has its own exposed architecture. To use a content management system, one must understand the basics of the particular system, and then comprehension and insight into how one performs development using that particular system. Hence, one can quickly start creating powerful and dynamic websites.

Advantages of content management systems

When using a content management system, often the only thing that is required to build the site is to let the system know what type of content you want, how you would like it to be displayed, and who can do what. Almost everything else is handled by the system. This allows the developer to focus on the key areas of any website, which are the content itself and its presentation.

Most content management systems come without the prerequisite of needing to know a programming language. Although knowledge of the language helps in many ways, one can still build powerful and custom sites without any prior experience. Moreover, all CMSs are so user-friendly with onscreen help and wizards, that you have all that you need to get started right in front of you. Perhaps, simplicity is the keyword for any CMS. Of course, the simplicity mentioned here is what is called pseudo-simplicity, where a complex system hides within itself all of the complexity but exposes a simple usability.

Content management systems come with the necessary demonstration templates and sample pages that can be used to quickly kickstart the website. In most CMSs, almost without any effort, you have the baseline to start with, and all that is left to do is customizing the site to your requirements.

Disadvantages of content management systems

Simple sites are alright, but when the requirement grows, creating everything with what is already available requires a new mindset. Often, the biggest hurdle that developers find in getting used to a content management system is that everything is defined as content and not objects or functions. So every component that is available for download speaks in terms of what it does with the content. It is often necessary to use multiple components to get what you need. This is the case with any well-abstracted system; it takes a new mindset to learn it!

Many CMSs introduce the requirement of some templating language to be able to customize the look and feel of the site. In such cases, there is an overhead of learning the templating language, as well as learning how to use the templating language to create a new look and feel within the CMS used.

A big disadvantage of a CMS is that you are restricted to the functionalities provided by the CMS. Depending on the exposed architecture, there could be practical limitations on the extendibility of the CMS. Certain CMSs cannot be extended much beyond what they already have to offer. Certain CMSs can be extended a little, but not by much more. Some CMSs can be extended, but only at the cost of learning complex APIs and methodologies that are specific to the CMS. There are also some CMSs that allow extendibility with just the knowledge of the programming language in which they were written.

Why MODx?

As the following diagram shows, MODx breaks the limitations that are generally found in CMSs and yet provides the simplicity necessary to quickly start developing.

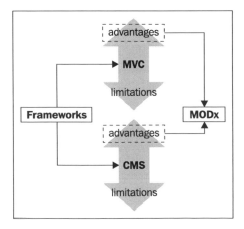

Why a CMS?

Content management systems are used when one wants to create a site that can be self-maintained. It really does replace a programmer for maintenance. The websites for most companies have simple workflows, if any. And there are a lot of individuals who would like to have a website for themselves, just like everyone wanted to have a business card. Content management systems avoid having to pay professional rates for simple websites when you can create and maintain such sites yourself. You might want to use a professional to initially create the website, but still maintain it yourself in order to provide a quicker turnaround time in updating new content. These are situations where a CMS like MODx provides a solution.

Why an application framework?

Application frameworks take over where the limitations of CMSs begin—when you want more than what is possible. To use any application framework, you must know the language it uses. But if you really want to develop, then you better be a programmer—but a smart one who lets the system handle "the obvious things"!

So, why MODx?

MODx provides the ease of a CMS and the extendibility of a framework, which is made possible by exposing a new architecture that is both easy and flexible. It is possible to create very complex and custom sites in MODx. Hence, one can start developing a complete site in MODx without any programming knowledge and use expertise only for the elements that need programming skills, if they are needed.

Another interesting concept of MODx is how it handles templating. Unlike most CMSs available, there is no need to learn any templating language in order to introduce a theme to your site. Hence, it does not even have the small learning curve of a templating language.

MODx is designed to be intuitive; hence, it is easy for anyone to understand how to create sites quickly and effectively. Once you have learned the basics, you will realize that the experience keeps getting better.

MODx administration is AJAX-driven, giving you the ability to manage the site with abilities that are very user friendly. Sites created with MODx can also have AJAX-enabled features without much effort. Many built-in snippets, such as the AJAX search snippet available for MODx, come with interesting AJAX functionalities that can be used out-of-the-box.

MODx is search-engine friendly, which means that it has everything to help you get your site listed on Google or any other famous search engine.

MODx is an open source project and, like most open source projects, it has strong community support. There are countless places from which to get help when you are stuck, and almost all queries get answered within a day. Moreover, having community support means that support will keep getting better.

All of this makes MODx suitable both for a casual developer who would like a quick site and also for serious developers who want something easy to start with and the option to build sophistication gradually. MODx uses an architecture that helps to overcome most of the disadvantages mentioned under application frameworks and CMSs while retaining their advantages.

Overview of the book

This book teaches you how to use MODx to create powerful, dynamic websites, even without the knowledge of a programming language. It leads you step-by-step, in a logical pattern, through building a complete website. Each chapter covers certain concepts, and includes simple examples. All of the examples, if you follow along, aggregate to a self-created website. The book also includes a chapter dedicated to the serious programmers who would like to extend what they can do with MODx.

This book can also be used as a reference or to relearn the particular concepts that have been discussed in each chapter. It has illustrative examples, wherever necessary, to make sure that it is friendly. It has a mixture of simple demonstrations and in-depth concepts that will interest both casual and serious readers.

Summary

In this chapter, you have learned the general concepts of web development and also been assured as to why MODx, as a tool, is a good choice for developing your website. The various development methodologies, especially a CMS and a Web Application, Framework have been explained. With these briefings on the fundamentals, you should have a clear understanding of what MODx is and why you would want to use it.

2
Getting Started

This chapter takes you through setting up and starting MODx. It also refers to the online documentation resources and discusses how to get community help. It sets the base for developing the example applications in this book.

Setting up the development environment

This section of the book will help you to install MODx and verify that it is working.

Prerequisites

The following is the list of software packages that have to be installed in order for MODx to work. If you have them installed and configured already, you can skip this section. Otherwise, you can read the instructions that are specific to your operating system.

- PHP
- MySQL
- Apache

MODx is built using PHP, which stands for PHP Hypertext Processor. PHP is a server-side language and we need a web server that can interpret PHP. We are using Apache, which is the most widely used web server for this. Apache is not really a prerequisite; any web server that can interpret PHP, such as IIS or Nginx, would do.

 MODx uses MySQL as the database server.

For the sake of simplicity and consistency of settings and configurations, throughout the book, we will be using a package called **XAMPP**, which bundles Apache, PHP, MySQL, and various tools to get you easily started with a local development environment.

This section explains how to set up the prerequisites for different OSs.

Linux

XAMPP for Linux is for download from `http://www.apachefriends.org/en/xampp-linux.html`.

Download the latest stable release available. You will get a file with a name in the format `xampp-linux-(version number).tar.gz`.

1. To begin installation, open a shell prompt, such as konsole or gterm.

2. Change the current directory to the directory to which you downloaded XAMPP. For example, if you have downloaded it to the desktop, you would type `cd ~/Desktop`.

3. To install XAMPP, you must have superuser rights. If you are not the superuser, type `su` followed by the password at the prompt to get root user permissions. Some operating systems, such as Ubuntu, do not have a superuser. In such a case, you must specify a prefix of `sudo` before the commands mentioned here.

4. Next, type `tar xvfz xampp-linux-(version number).tar.gz -C /opt`. If you have done everything properly so far, then you will have XAMPP successfully installed.

5. To start the XAMPP server, type `/opt/lampp/lampp start`. If XAMPP has been started successfully, you will see a response like this: **LAMPP started**.

> The Linux version of XAMPP was previously called LAMPP and so you may see LAMPP where you expected XAMPP.

Windows

XAMPP for Windows is available for download at `http://www.apachefriends.org/en/xampp-windows.html`. Download the version that is packaged as a Windows Installer file, as it is easier to set up.

Run the set-up file and choose the installation directory. After a successful installation, you will see a small icon in the taskbar that lists the enabled services. Make sure that Apache and MySQL are running. If they are not, click on the **Start** button next to the Apache and MySQL services. Your Windows firewall might ask if you want to block these services. If asked to do so, click on the **Unblock** button.

 Note that here we are using XAMPP only to make things simpler for you to get started. You can use any web server that supports PHP, including IIS.

MAC

MAMP is the easiest way to get started on a MAC machine. It can be downloaded from `http://www.mamp.info/en/mamp.html` and installed like any other MAC application.

Verification

To verify that the installation is working, open the browser and type `http://localhost`. You will see a page similar to the example shown in the following screenshot, if everything is installed correctly.

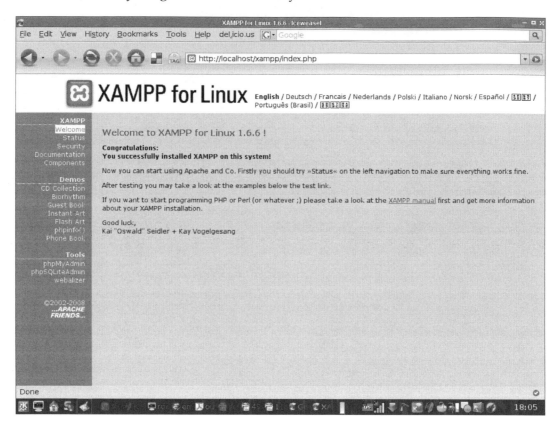

The following screenshot shows the MAMP screen for the MAC:

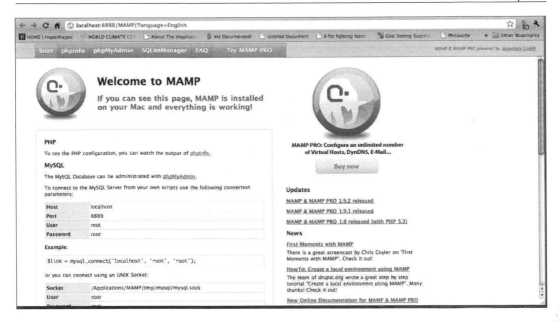

Downloading MODx

MODx is available for download from the site `http://MODxcms.com/downloads.html`. Make sure that you download MODx Evolution and not MODx Revolution. MODx is distributed under the GNU General Public License which, on a lighter note, means that you can download it for free, install it on as many sites as you like, and even modify and redistribute it under a new name. For more information about the license, refer to `http://MODxcms.com/license.html`.

Like most open source projects, MODx has a stable release and a preview beta release. The stable release is what has been tested and made ready for production. For any production use, you must be using the stable version. The preview and beta release is to test out new features and possibly identify any bugs, in the process of using it. There is also a development snapshot that can be checked out (downloaded) from the SVN repository (`http://MODxcms.com/svn.html`) as the developers make changes.

For this book, we will be using the stable version. The stable version at the time of writing was MODx Evolution 1.0.4. Click on the link that allows you to download the stable version, and unzip it using any ZIP utility that your operating system supports, such as WinZip, WinRAR, or TAR.

Installing MODx

Unzip the downloaded archive and place it in a folder named learningMODx within the root directory of your web server. This should be a directory named www or htdocs, under your Apache or XAMPP installation.

Possible root folders are as follows, depending on the installation:

- /var/www/
- /opt/xampp/htdocs/
- c:\program files\xampp\htdocs

Next, open http://localhost/learningMODx. If everything is fine so far, you should see something like the example shown in the following screenshot:

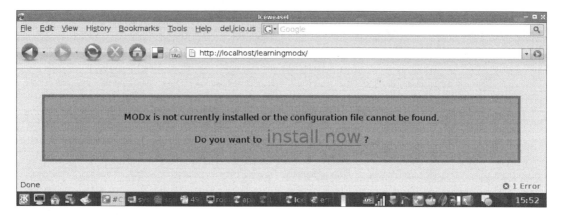

Creating a database

MODx needs one database to store all of the data. This database must have been created, and the username and password of a user who has privileges to read from and write to the database must be given.

MODx can create the database for you if the MySQL user that you specify in the set-up page has permissions to create the specified database.

With the default installation of XAMPP, there is only one user with the name root for MySQL, and it is not a good idea to use this user for MODx or any similar platforms. This is because the database username and password are stored in plain text files and someone with access to just MODx files can bring down all of the databases, sometimes even unintentionally.

There are two methods to get the database configured:

- You can define a user and grant that user privileges to create a database. In such a case, MODx can use that user and create the database for you.

- You can create the database and the user yourself.

In this example, we will create both the user and the database. phpMyAdmin comes along with XAMPP and is not related to MODx.

1. In a new browser page, open `http://localhost/phpmyadmin`.

2. Click on the **Privileges** link, and then click on **Add a new user**.

3. On the new user page, for the purpose of this book, create the username as **learningMODx**, give the password as **m0dxdbus3r**, make sure you select the option **Create database with same name and grant all privileges**, and then click on **Go**.

Here, we have created a user called **learningMODx** and a database with the same name, and we have granted all privileges on this database to that user.

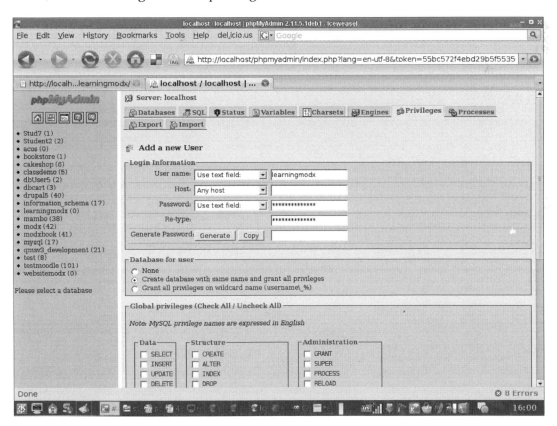

If you are familiar with MySQL, you can also do the same with the following query, using your MySQL client:

```
create database learningMODx;
grant usage on *.* to learningMODx@localhost identified by
                                        'learniningMODx';
grant all privileges on learningMODx.* to learningMODx@localhost ;
```

Starting the installation

The next step is to go to the page `http://localhost/learningMODx`. Click on **Install now**.

1. Select the language, and then click on **NEXT**.

2. You will be asked about what you want the installer to do. For a site that is not yet installed, a new installation option button will be the only option enabled. Click on the **Next** button.

3. You will see a page like the one shown in the following screenshot:

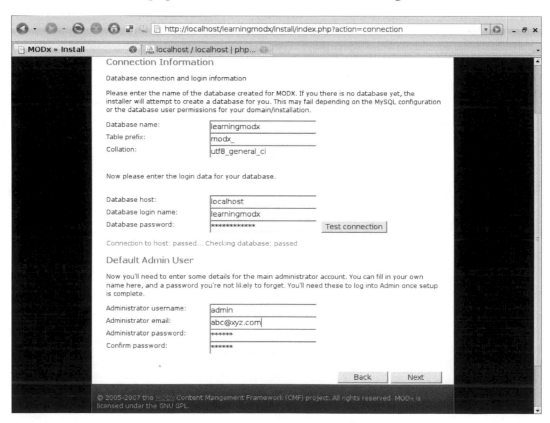

4. Enter the appropriate information into the following fields:

    °   **Database host**: The hostname or IP address of the machine where the SQL server is installed. If you are running it from a local machine, this could be **localhost**. If you are using MAMP, or if for any other reason the MySQL server is running on a port other than the default port (3306), you will have to specify the port number after the hostname, separated by a colon. For example, **localhost:8889**.

    °   **Database login name**: Set this field to the username that we created: **learningMODx**.

    °   **Database password**: Set this field to the password that you gave during creation (**m0dxdbus3r**).

    °   **Test connection**: After entering the preceding details, check that the database connectivity is working by clicking on **Test connection**. This will show a small label (**passed - collations now available**), indicating whether or not the connection succeeded.

5. Once the test connection is successful, you will see the following additional fields:

    °   **Database name**: The database that MODx must use. Specify the name of the new database that we have created: **learningMODx**.

    °   **Table prefix**: MODx creates a lot of tables in the database. Having a prefix for these tables will allow you to have more than one installation of MODx in the same database. This could be useful when using a shared host where you can only have a limited number of databases. For the purpose of this chapter, you can leave this field with the default value of **modx_**.

    °   **Connection Method**: This is best left to its default value, unless you have a specific reason for changing it.

    °   **Collation**: You can change this to include other character sets for your database, if you like.

6. Next, click on **Create or test selection of your database**, and you will see the following section, along with a message stating **Checking database: passed - database selected**.

    °   **Default Admin User**: MODx allows the user to manage the site from a frontend manager interface, without having to look into the code or database. We will call this interface the manager interface. The **Default Admin User** can log in to the manager interface. Fill in the fields with the relevant details for this user, and remember the username and password so that you can administer the site. Select the **Default Manager Language**, and then proceed with the installation by clicking **NEXT**.

You will see a page like the example shown in the following screenshot:

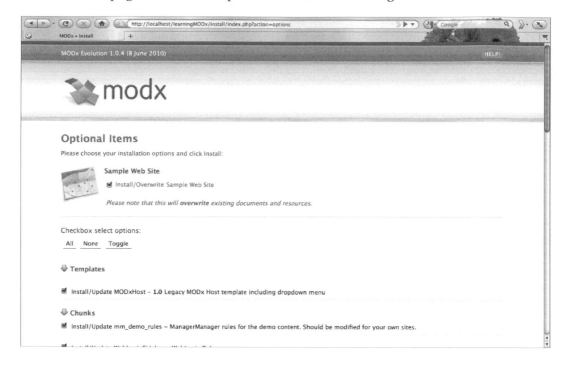

The next step is to select all of the checkboxes on the next page, and continue with the installation. Make sure that you select the checkbox next to **Install/Overwrite Sample Web Site**. Also, select all of the elements by clicking on the **All** link beneath the text **Checkbox select options**. These checkboxes tell MODx to install all of the available elements and a sample site. It is not necessary in a production environment to select all of the options, especially not the sample web site. Here we are installing everything so that we can also learn by looking at the existing content, once we are familiar with the basics. Most of the elements that are selected here will be explained in detail in the later chapters of this book. If you haven't already, continue with the installation by clicking on **INSTALL**.

Installation status and diagnostics

The next page performs a check to ensure that everything is working correctly. You will see something like the example shown in the following screenshot:

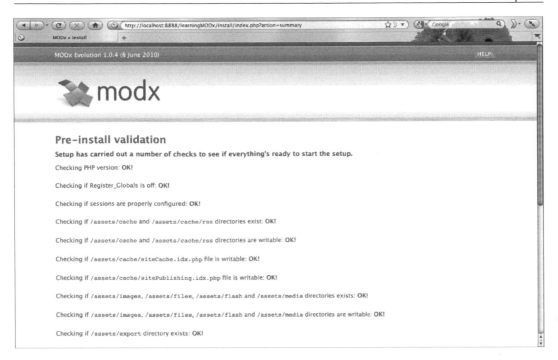

You may get errors due to permissions on certain folders that need to be writable. In such a case, you will see messages in red describing which folders have to be writable but are not. The folders that require write permission during installation are `assets/cache`, `assests/images`, and `assests/export`. In Windows systems, this can be changed by right-clicking on the respective folders and choosing the appropriate permissions. In Linux systems, use the following command to change permissions:

```
$chmod -R 0666 (foldername)
```

You might also be required to create a file named `config.inc.php` in the `manager/includes/` folder, with writable permissions. This file gets written automatically most of the time, but in some server environments that use IIS, it will not be possible to do so. If the web server has write permissions for the folder `manager/includes/`, then MODx will create `config.inc.php` automatically. However, this is not a good security practice.

At the bottom of the page, you will see a checkbox next to the text **I agree to the terms of the MODx license**. Select this checkbox to accept the license terms, and then, click on **INSTALL** in order to proceed with the installation. If you encounter any errors on this page related to the database, you may want to start the installation again, after verifying your database credentials.

You will then see an **Installation Successful** page with an option to delete the `install` folder. It is a good security practice to always delete this folder after installation. You don't want someone trying to reinstall your site, although he or she may not get very far without knowing your database access details.

After installation of the demo site, visit `http://localhost/learningMODx` and you will see a page similar to the example shown in the following screenshot:

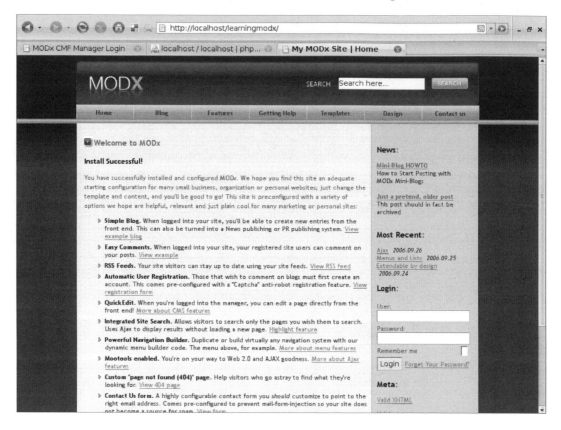

Also, make sure that you are able to log in with the default admin user that you created. Open `http://localhost/learningMODx/manager` and type in your default admin username and password. After a successful login, you will see a page similar to the example shown in the following screenshot:

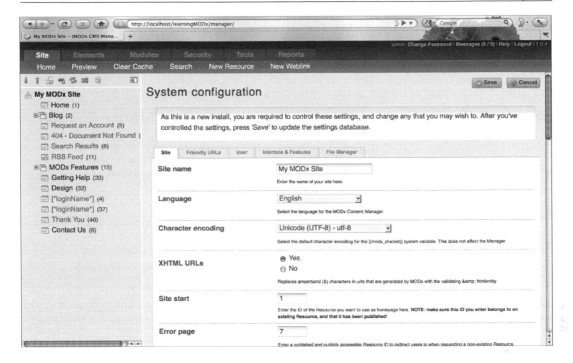

Congratulations! If you have reached this point so far and can see the screen shown in the previous screenshot, it means that you have successfully installed MODx with the demo site, and are all set to start learning and developing by following the instructions in this book.

Documentation

The most important resource for learning any open source technology is the documentation that it comes bundled with. This section introduces you to the available documentation for MODx.

There are three kinds of documentation available:

- Official documentation
- Community-driven documentation
- Combined

Official documentation

The official documentation for MODx is available from the official MODx site at http://MODxcms.com/documentation.html. The official documentation tries to contain as much text as possible to cover everything about MODx. However, due to the rapid level at which changes happen, and the process involved in making documentation official, the official documentation does not cover everything. You can be assured that whatever is covered in there is free from error, and can be a very good resource to start with, but, as you progress with MODx, you will find that there are other forms of documentation that are more interesting.

Community-driven documentation

Community-driven documentation is those write-ups and aggregated knowledge that are shared among MODx users. The MODx wiki and MODx forums contain a wealth of community-driven documents. Although the MODx wiki has not caught up with the pace of the project's progression yet, it still has some useful documentation. You can access the MODx wiki at http://Wiki.MODxcms.com. The MODx forum is very active. When you are stuck with a situation and need to know if someone has already cracked it for you, it helps to do a search of the forum first. Many concepts that have already been cracked are available as small how-to. For many snippets that you might be using, you will also find a support thread in the forums to make it easier for you to learn more about the snippet and read about what other users have experienced already. The MODx forums can be accessed at http://MODxcms.com/forums/index.php.

Combined

There is effort going on to build a more structured and collated documentation system, along with a search facility. Please be sure to check the documentation at http://rtfm.modx.com/display/Evo1/Home.

Getting support

What happens when you are stuck and have already searched the forums, have tried Googling, and still you haven't found a solution to your problem? That's when you can use the community to get interactive support. There are two common means of interactive support, the forums and **IRC (Internet Relay Chat)**.

Before we discuss forums and IRC, the following is a list of guidelines one must always remember in order to get helpful replies:

- Before asking, thoroughly check to see if what you are asking has already been answered in the forums.

- Don't ask to ask. That is, do not ask questions like "Can I post a question?"

- Be specific with your questions. Always make sure that when you are asking a question, you explain the following:
    - What you tried
    - What result you expected
    - What result you saw instead

- Know your terminology. It is easier to be precise when you know the correct terminology to use when asking your question.

- Be patient! Sometimes it may take a while before someone notices your questions and posts an answer.

- Always use a pastebin service when posting large lines of code. These are services that allow you to post code, and that give you a URL in return that you can use to share the code with others. One such pastebin service is `www.rafb.net/paste/`. Use such services when posting code in order to maintain uncluttered continuity of the conversation.

- Capital casing and red coloring are considered to be shouting.

- Ask the question in the related room or thread.

- Remember, a well-formed question is half answered. Your response is directly related to the kind of questions that you ask. There is a tutorial written on how to ask questions the smart way. It can be accessed at `http://catb.org/~esr/faqs/smart-questions.html`. Reading this tutorial really helps a lot in getting community help.

Web forums

You need to register on the forums before you can post queries. You can register at `http://modxcms.com/forums/`.

The MODx forum is just like any other forum, where you can post your queries and can expect them to be answered. If you cannot find any other suitable threads, then the thread **Support | General Support** is a good place to put your queries.

IRC

Most open source projects have IRC communities supporting the project. MODx has one too. To be able to use the IRC service, you need an IRC client. The most popular IRC client for Windows is **mIRC**, which can be downloaded from http:// www.mirc.com/. In Linux, all of the famous instant messengers, such as pidgin and kopete, support IRC. IRC has the concepts of servers and channels. When you connect to a server, you may join the channels available on that server. MODx has a channel #MODx for itself in the server irc.freenode.org. This channel is only for MODx-specific questions. If you have a question that is related to PHP, it will be answered in the #php channel on the same server.

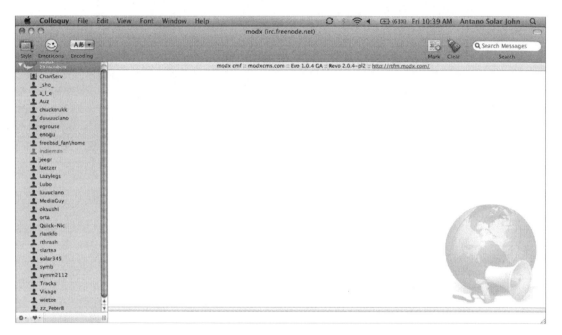

Summary

In this chapter, you have learned how to set up a working platform for developing websites with MODx that includes the installation and configuration of the prerequisites, such as Apache, PHP, and MySQL. To make the process easier, you have used XAMPP, which is a bundle containing all of these packages. Finally, you have installed MODx and have verified that everything is set and ready.

3
MODx Basics

In this chapter, you will learn the basics of MODx, and how to create a Front Page for the site. The basic elements explained in this chapter are:

- Site configurations
- Documents and containers
- The Manager interface
- The TinyMCE editor

Site configuration

When you first log in to the MODx Manager interface, you will see the site configuration page in the rightmost panel. Here, you can customize some basic configurations of the site. You can reach this page from anywhere in the MODx Manager by clicking on the **Configuration** sub-menu in the **Tools** menu.

All of the options that can be configured from this Configuration page are settings that are global to the entire site. After changing the configurations, you have to let MODx store them by clicking on the **Save** button.

The following is the screenshot of the Configuration page:

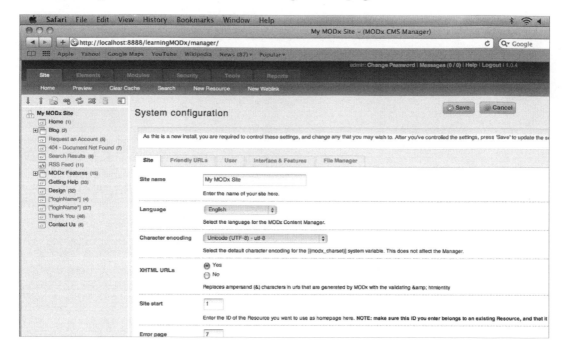

The configurations are grouped into five categories:

- **Site**—mostly, settings that are used to personalize the site
- **Friendly URLs**—settings to help make the site search-engine optimized
- **User**—settings related to user logins
- **Interface & Features**—mostly, Manager interface customizations
- **File Manager**—settings defining what can be uploaded and where

Configuring the site

In this section, we are going to make a few changes to get you familiar with the various configurations available. We will learn what some of the other configurations do as we proceed through the book. Most configurations have tooltips that describe them in a little pop-up when you move the mouse over them.

Default Manager interface page

After making changes in the site configuration and saving it, you will be redirected to another page. This page is available by clicking on the **Home** link on the **Site** tab. This page is also the default Manager interface page. This means that every time you log in using the Manager login screen, you will reach this page by default.

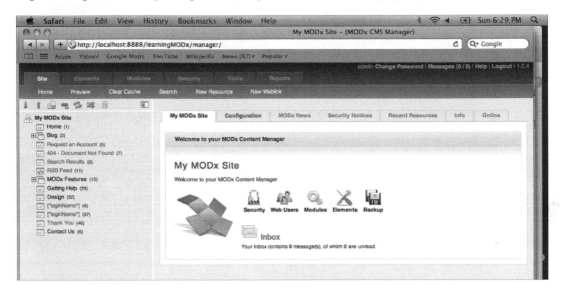

This page has seven tabs, which are briefly explained below:

- **My MODx Site**: Provides quick access to certain features in MODx.

- **Configuration**: Displays information on the current status of the site.

- **MODx News**: Shows updates on what is happening with MODx.

- **Security Notices**: Shows updates on what is happening with MODx that is specific to security.

- **Recent Resources**: Shows a list with hyperlinks of the recently created or edited resources.

- **Info**: Shows information about your login status.

- **Online**: Lists all of the active users.

Noticing and fixing errors and warnings

The **Configuration** tab of the default Manager interface page displays errors and warnings about issues in the installation, if any. Generally, it also has instructions on how to fix them. Most of the time, the warnings are for security issues or suggestions for improving performance. Hence, although the site will continue to work when there are warnings listed on this page, it is good practice to fix the issues that have caused these warnings.

Here we discuss three such warnings that occur commonly, and also show how to fix them.

- `config` file still writable: This is shown when the `config` file is still writable. It can be fixed by changing the properties of the configuration file to read only.

- `register_globals` is set to **ON** in your `php.ini` configuration file: This is a setting in the PHP configuration file. This should be set to **OFF**. Having it **ON** makes the site more vulnerable to what is known as **cross site scripting** (**XSS**).

- **Configuration warning**—GD and/or Zip PHP extensions not found: This is shown when you do not have the specified packages installed with PHP. MAMP doesn't come with the ZIP extension and you can ignore this configuration if you are not using it in production. Both XAMPP and MAMP come with the GD extension by default.

Changing the name of the site

In the previous section, we listed the groups of configuration options that are available. Let us change one option—the name of the site—now.

1. Click on the **Tools** menu in the top navigational panel
2. Click on the **Configuration Menu** item
3. Change the text field labeled **Site Name** to **Learning MODx**
4. Click on the **Save** button

The basic element of MODx: Resources

Resources are the basic building blocks in MODx. They are the elements that make up the content of the site. Every web page in MODx corresponds to a Resource page. In early versions of MODx, Resources were called Documents. Thinking of them as documents may make it easier for you to understand. Every resource has a unique ID. This ID can be passed along in the URL, and MODx will display the page for the resource with the same ID. In the simplest case, a resource contains plain text.

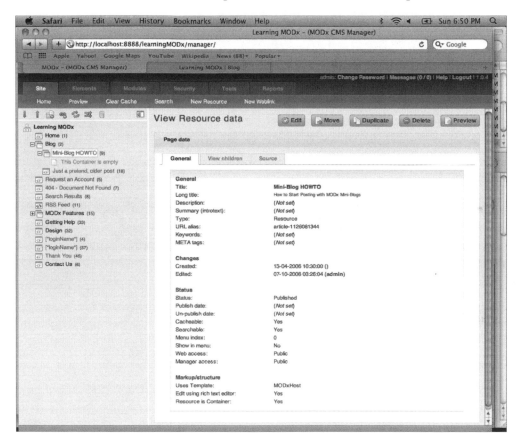

As can be seen from the previous screenshot, the ID referred to here is 2, and the content displayed on the screen is from resource ID 9. It is also possible to refer to a resource by an alias name instead of an ID. An **alias** is a friendly name that can be used instead of having to use numbers. Aliases will be explained in more detail later in the book.

Containers

Resources can be contained within other resources called containers. Containers in MODx are like folders in filesystems, but with the difference that a container is also a resource. This means that every container also has a resource ID, and a corresponding page is shown when such an ID is referenced in the URL.

MODx Manager interface

MODx is administered and customized by using the provided Manager interface. From the Manager interface, you can edit resources, place them within containers, and change their properties. You can log in to the **Manager** interface by using the Manager login screen `http://sitename/manager`, by using the username and password that you supplied when installing MODx. The Manager interface is divided into two panes. The leftmost pane always displays the resources in a resource tree, and the rightmost pane displays the content relevant to your last action.

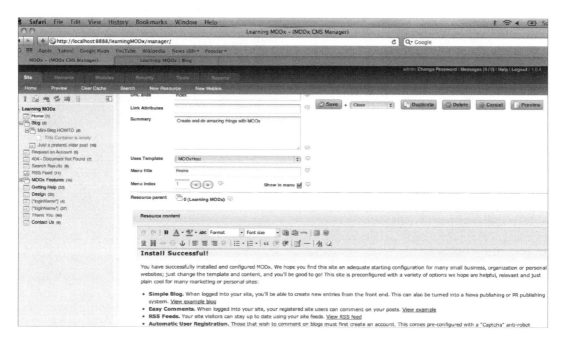

The two preceding panes you see are the menu and the corresponding menu items. Each of these leads to the different functionalities of MODx.

In the leftmost pane, you will see the site name followed by a hierarchically-grouped resource list. There is a **+** near every unexpanded container that has other resources. When you click on the **+** symbol, the container expands to show the children and the **+** symbol changes to a **–** symbol. Clicking on the **–** symbol hides the children of the respective container. The resource's ID is displayed in parentheses after the resource's title in the resource tree.

The top of leftmost pane consists of a few icons, referred to as the Resource Toolbar, which help to control the visibility of the resource tree.

- **Expand Site Tree** — expand all of the containers to show their children and siblings.
- **Collapse Site Tree** — collapse all of the containers to hide their children and siblings.
- **New Resource** — open a new resource page in the rightmost pane.
- **New Weblink** — open a new weblink page in the rightmost pane.
- **Refresh Site Tree** — refresh the tree of containers and resources to make available any changes that are not yet reflected in the tree.
- **Sort the Site Tree** — open a pop-up page where you can select from the various criteria available to sort the tree.
- **Purge** — when you delete a resource, it stays in the recycle bin. The resources are struck out with a red line. The resources can be completely removed from the system by clicking on the **Purge** icon.
- **Hide Site Tree** — this icon slides the leftmost pane out of view, giving more space for the rightmost pane.

Right-clicking on a resource brings up a context menu from where you can perform various actions on the resource. Clicking on **Edit** will open the page for editing in the rightmost pane. The context menu provides interesting shortcuts that are very handy.

Using the HTML editor

MODx is bundled with a **What You See Is What You Get (WYSIWYG)** editor. So resources can be edited and modified without having to know HTML. This section shows you how to use the editor.

To edit any resource, click on the corresponding resource in the leftmost pane, and then click on **Edit**. Scroll down until you see the section with the title **Resource Content**. Here, you can edit the document using any installed text editor, or you can edit it as plain HTML. You can toggle this option by selecting the appropriate method from the editor by using the drop-down box. With the default installation, you have two choices—**TinyMCE** for a WYSIWYG editor and **None** for editing plain HTML.

This section discusses the TinyMCE editor that we installed during the MODx installation process. TinyMCE is open source software provided by http://tinymce.moxiecode.com.

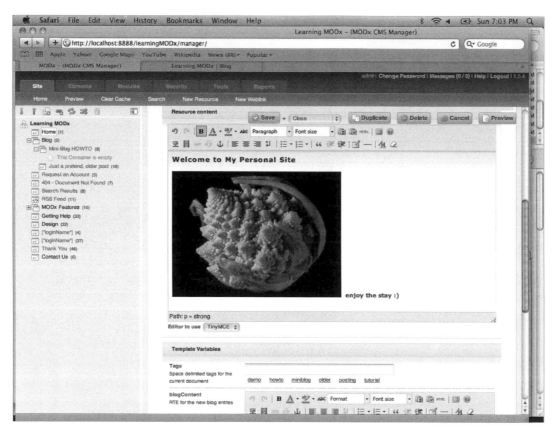

The TinyMCE editor comes with handy tools to make the editing of your resources easier. It has small buttons on the top that you can click to perform the appropriate actions. Moving the mouse cursor over these buttons brings up tooltips that display the name of the button and the keyboard shortcut, if any. Using the keyboard shortcut can be handy when you are required to use a button multiple times. The available buttons, and many other settings, can be changed from the site configuration that was discussed earlier.

Notice that if you do not see the image. Click on the HTML icon in TinyMCE, and if you see additional quotes, you may want to turn off Magic Quotes, as mentioned in `http://modxcms.com/forums/index.php?topic=40996.0`.

Creating the Front Page

Now, you should understand what resources are and how the Manager interface allows you to create and control them. We will now create a Front Page.

In the Manager page, perform the following steps:

1. Right-click on the **Resource** with ID 1 in the leftmost panel
2. Click on **Edit** and fill in the following details:
   - **Title: Home**
   - **Long title: Welcome to Learning MODx**
   - **Description: My Personal Site using MODx**
   - **Summary: The welcome page to my visitors**
   - **Uses template: MODxHost**
3. Insert some content that you would like to have in the Front Page, replacing the existing content from the demo site.

4. Click on **Save**.

5. Click on the **Preview** menu item in the **Site** menu to open a preview of the site in a new window.

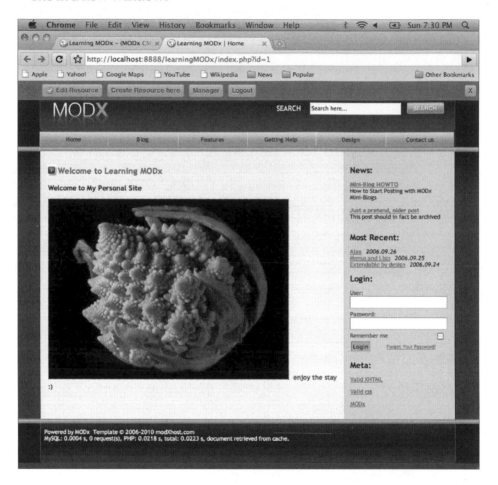

You might want to change the entire content of your Home Page instead of just the content area. We will introduce templates in the next chapter, which will allow you to make all of your content have a consistent and interesting look.

When editing resources, it is good practice to save your changes frequently. Because you are editing the resources through the website, if you take too long before you save, then the page will get timed out, which will result in the loss of any changes that you had made.

DocManager module

If you move the mouse to the top of the page, as shown in the following screenshot, you will notice four buttons: **Edit Resource**, **Create Resource here**, **Manager**, and **Logout**.

Edit Resource and **Create Resource here** are available to quickly edit and create resources, respectively, without having to go back to the Manager interface. The **Manager** button takes you back to the **Manager** interface and **Logout** logs you out from the manager interface.

These functionalities are available when you:

- Log in as an admin from the Manager page, then open a new tab or new window, and then visit any page in the site
- Click on **Preview Resource** from within the Manager interface

When you click on **Edit Resource**, it opens up a pop-up page where you can edit the Resource details.

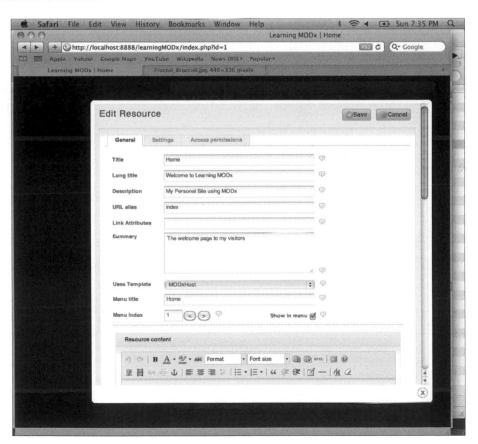

Once you make changes to the resource in the pop-up window, you can see the changes in the original page by clicking on the **Update** button. When you are done with editing the content, click on the **Close** button denoted by **x** at the lower-right of the window, or by clicking on the **Cancel** button.

Resources revisited

This section gives more information on resources and their properties.

Editing documents

A document has many properties attached to it. Changing the values of these properties changes the behavior of the document. When you click on **Edit** after clicking on a resource, you will see the following options next to the save button:

- **Add another** — creates a new document after saving the current document
- **Continue editing** — remains on the same page, even after saving the current document
- **Close** — closes the current page after saving the document

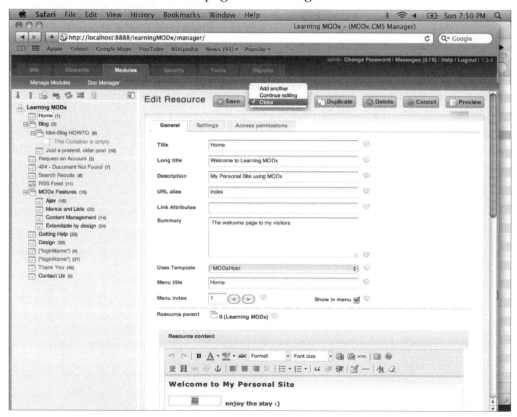

Resource properties

The following are the Resource properties:

General tab

- **Title**: The title of the resource. This is generally a short title that gets displayed when listing your resources.

- **Long title**: The long title of the resource. This is a more descriptive title of the resource.

- **Description**: Here, you can set the optional description of the resource.

- **URL alias**: When friendly URLs are enabled, the resources can be accessed by using a friendly name, called the alias, instead of the ID. Here, you can set the resource's alias.

- **Link Attributes**: When this resource is opened through a link, you might want it to open in a relative window. Here, you can specify the relative targets for the link.

- **Summary (Introtext)**: A brief summary of the resource can be specified here, depending on whether or not your templates use the summary. More of the resource properties that are used in the templates are explained in the next chapter.

- **Uses template**: Set the template within which the resource's content will be used. Templates are explained in detail in the next chapter.

- **Menu title**: Here you can specify the title that you would like to use as a menu item if your resource is accessible from a menu. If no menu title is set for the page, the page title will be used.

- **Menu index**: Menus can be generated in MODx dynamically. This is explained in detail in the chapter on menus (*Chapter 7, Creating Lists*). **Menu index** allows you to have fine control over the ordering of the menu. For example, menus can be sorted in ascending or descending order of the menu index. **Menu index** is a number assigned to the resource to allow this fine control over dynamically-generated menus.

- **Resource parent**: Resources can be organized to be within containers. A resource parent is the container within which you would like this resource to be. To select the resource parent, click on the small gray icon next to this field, and then click on the document that you would like to have as the parent document.

Settings

This page provides checkboxes to enable or disable certain properties, some of which we have already discussed. The list of these checkboxes is:

- **Published**
- **Container**
- **Rich text**
- **Enable Stats Tracking**
- **Searchable**
- **Cacheable**

In addition to the checkboxes listed above, you also have the following fields available to you:

- **Publish date**: You can use this field to publish the document on a future date. You can select the publishing date by clicking on the *calendar* icon next to this field. You can remove the publishing date by clicking on the icon next to it.

- **Un-publish date**: This is similar to the previous field, but it unpublishes (removes from availability) the page on the specified date.

- **Resource Type**: You can choose whether the resource is a Web Page or a Weblink. Weblinks are explained later in this book.

- **Internet Media Type**: You can choose whether the resource contains HTML or XML, Microsoft Word documents, and so on.

- **Empty cache**: If you want MODx to clear the current cache of the document, leave this field selected. Once you save the document properties, the cache is cleared for this document and this field is cleared.

- **Content Disposition**: This is a drop-down box with two options:
    - **Inline**: When the document is accessed, its contents are rendered by the browser.
    - **Attachment**: When the document is accessed, its contents are available for download as a file.

Access permissions

Here, you define who has access to the documents. More on this is covered in *Chapter 5, Authentication and Authorization*.

Summary

In this chapter, you have learned about resources and containers and how every page that is displayed gets its content from a resource. You have also learned to create, edit, and manipulate resources and manage their configurations, and have also received an explanation of the TinyMCE editor. This chapter also explained each and every configuration option available for documents, and also the general configurable options of the site. Finally, you created a Front Page using what you have learned, and were introduced to the convenience of the DocManager.

4
Templating

Templates are the HTML layout within which a requested resource's content is displayed. Templates can themselves be dynamic and can have different elements that show different things, depending on various factors. The content of a template includes dynamic data, whereas the same template shows different content, depending on the resource requested. In this chapter, you will learn about templates and the elements that make dynamic content possible in templates. These are called template variables.

Changing the template of a resource

If you have followed along and have created the front page from the previous example, your website will look like the following screenshot:

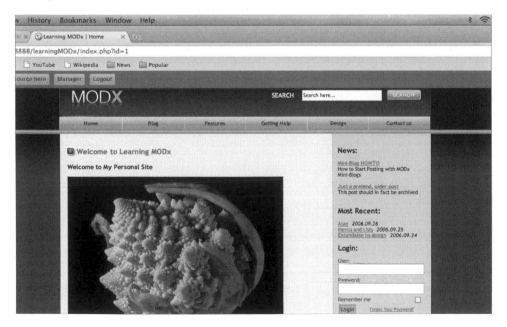

Now, to get a practical feel of what templates are all about, let us go ahead and change the template of the home page to none. You will immediately notice that all of the menus and layouts have disappeared and only the content of the resource is shown. Later in the chapter, we will go on to create our own template.

Follow these steps to modify the template of the home page to none:

1. Log in to the Manager interface as admin.

2. Click on the **Home** resource in the resource tree.

3. Click on **Edit** and change the option **Uses template** to **(blank)**. The document editing page will be refreshed, but the change to the document is not yet saved.

4. You may see a warning about losing previous publishing dates. Click on **Yes** to continue.

5. Click on **Save** to save the changes.

6. Click on **Preview** to see how the modified home page looks.

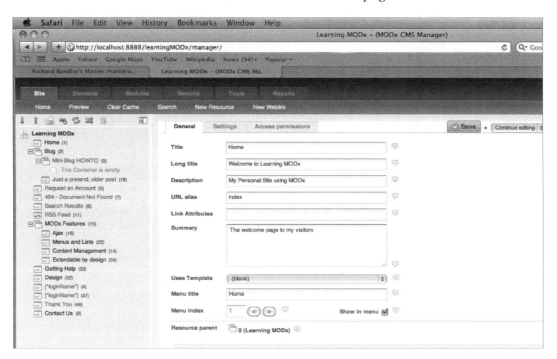

Now the home page will look similar to the following screenshot:

We have asked MODx to not use a template for the front page. Hence, the contents of the resource are rendered as such without being embedded within any other HTML structure. Earlier, we used the MODxHost template and the output was quite different.

We are now going to create a template of our own, by using simple HTML, and will make our resource use this template. This will explain the process of creating a template and also how to mark a portion within the template as the area in which to render the contents of the document.

Creating a new template and giving it a category

To start with, let us create a simple template that has a content area, a header, and a footer.

The HTML and CSS code for a structure like that is discussed in this section.

HTML

The following HTML creates a header, body, and footer layout. The `content div` is where the content of a resource will be displayed.

```
<!DOCTYPE html PUBLIC "-//W3C//DTD XHTML 1.1//EN" "http://www.w3.org/
TR/xhtml11/DTD/xhtml11.dtd"> <html
  xmlns="http://www.w3.org/1999/xhtml" xml:lang="en">
```

```
<head>
<title>Learning MODx</title>
<meta http-equiv="Content-Type" content="text/html; charset=iso-8859-
                                                               1" />
<link rel="stylesheet" type="text/css" href="assets/templates/
learningMODx/style.css" />
</head>
<body>
<div id="banner">
<h1>Learning MODx</h1>
</div>
<div id="wrapper">
  <div id="container">
    <div id="content">
      [*#content*] <!-- This is the only line that is not HTML.It is
                   explained in the sections below. -->
    </div>
  </div>
<div class="clearing"> </div>
</div> <!-- end of wrapper div -->
<div id="footer">It is fun and exciting to build websites with
                                          MODx</div></body>
</html>
```

CSS

The following CSS adds colors, borders, and padding to the preceding HTML layout:

```
* { padding:2; margin:0; border:1; }
body { margin:0 20px; background:#8CEC81; }
#banner { background: #2BB81B; border-top:5px solid #8CEC81; border-
bottom:5px solid #8CEC81; }
#banner h1 { padding:10px; }
#wrapper { background: #8CEC81; }
#container { width: 100%; background: #2BB81B; float: left; }
#content { background: #ffffff; height:600px; padding:10px; }
#footer { background: #2BB81B; border-top:5px solid #8CEC81; border-
bottom:5px solid #8CEC81; }
.clearing { clear:both; height:0; }
```

This book assumes that the reader is already familiar with HTML and CSS. As you will see, MODx makes it possible to use static HTML and CSS to be converted into dynamic templates.

Steps to create the new template

Let us use the preceding HTML to create a new template. For now, we will use this template to display our documents:

1. Click on the **Elements Menu** in the top navigation panel from within the Manager interface.

2. Click on the **Manage Elements** submenu.

3. The **Templates** tab is selected by default; if it is not, click on it.

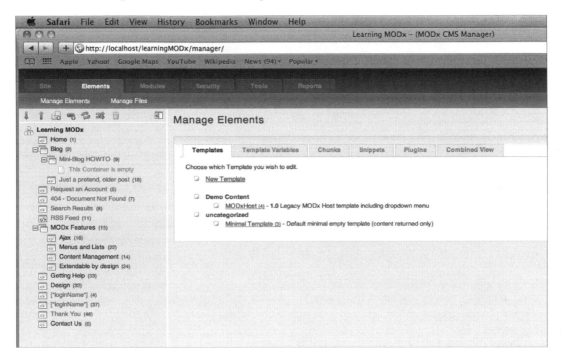

4. Click on **New Template**. You will see a screen like the one shown in the following screenshot:

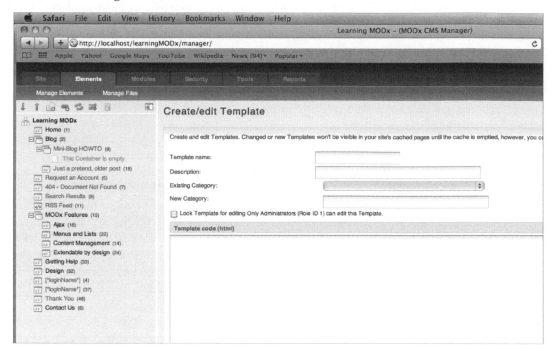

The following is an explanation of the various fields:

- **Template name** — name of the template to be created.

- **Description** — a friendly description to help you remember what the template is for, when you come back to your code later.

- **Existing Category** — one or more templates and other resources in MODx can be grouped together for personal organization. This will make it easier to remember which template to edit when you have a lot of them. From this drop-down, you can use an already-existing category.

- **New Category** — the same concept as the above field. When you enter a value in this field, a new category is created and the template is assigned to that category.

 Description and **Category** are there to just help you remember and group the templates when you want to use or edit them later. Their values don't affect any output of the site.

For the sake of this example, insert the following values into the aforementioned fields:

Name	Value
Template name	**Learning MODx default template**
Description	**The default template to use for the whole site**
Existing Category	[There will not be any values here yet]
New Category	**Learning MODx**
Template Code	Type in the HTML given in the *HTML* section

Now click on **Save** to create the new template. Because our template uses an external CSS file, we need to create a file called `style.css` and save it with the CSS content given in the CSS section.

As you can see from the HTML code, we are using this CSS file for our template.

We can save the CSS file anywhere, but it is always good to stick to conventions and store it in the `assets/templates/templatename` folder (`assets/templates/learningMODx/`), within the root of the MODx installation. In our example, the root of the MODx installation is the `htdocs/learningMODx` folder. We will, henceforth, refer to this folder as the **MODx root folder**.

It is also important to mention the same path when referring to the CSS in the template, as we have done earlier. All files are served from the MODx root folder because every page is actually rendered by `index.php`, which is stored in the MODx root folder.

Here is the relevant extract from the code given in the *HTML* section:

```
<link rel="stylesheet" type="text/css" href="assets/templates/
learningMODx/style.css" />
```

Notice the use of `[*#content*]` in the preceding HTML. We will discuss this in the next section. For now, just understand that when MODx parses `[*#content*]`, the content of the resource is placed in its position within the template, and hence it (`[*#content*]`) is called a **placeholder**.

> You can directly create the CSS file in the specified path or you can upload it by using the `Manage Files` menu item in the `Elements` menu.

Making the home page use the created template

Now that you have created a new template, let us use this template for the home page. The steps to change the template are the same as the ones mentioned in the *Changing the template of a resource* section. In that section, we changed the template of the resource to blank; this time, choose the template named Learning MODx, which is the default template, instead of blank.

Click on **Preview**, and the page will look similar to the one shown in the following screenshot:

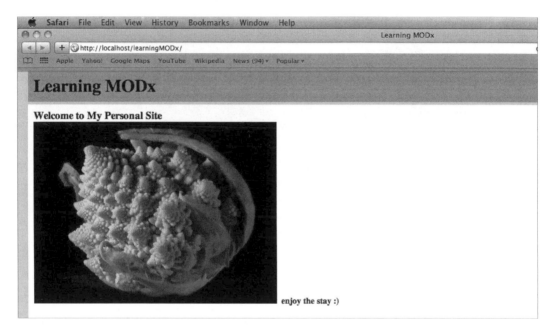

Choosing a default template

Now that we have made the home page use the newly-created template, we might also want to use this template for most of our other pages. Let us configure MODx to use this template as the default template for all documents that will henceforth be created:

1. Open the MODx site configuration, as explained in the previous chapter (**Tools | Configuration**).
2. Change the option **Default Template** in the drop-down box to the newly-created template.
3. Click on the **Save** button.

Introducing template variables

Template variables give life to otherwise static layouts. They allow templates to have dynamic content. You have already seen an example of a resource-specific template variable when you used [*#content*] in the template that you created in the last section. Template variables are entities that may have different values in different pages for different users at different times. They can be embedded in a template or in a resource's content, in order to display the value that they store. The value of a template variable can generally be shown in a template by enclosing the name of the template variable within [* and *], like [*template variable name*]. This is a good time to check out the code of the templates that came with the sample site when MODx was installed, in order to consolidate your understanding of what is happening. Template variables are created and assigned to documents, as we will see in the next section.

Besides the template variables that are explicitly created, all resources have certain values that are accessible as resource-specific variables. These variables contain information about the resource, such as the content of the resource, its name, description, who it was created by, and so on.

Modifying the template to add dynamic behavior

We have now created the template that renders the content of the resource at a specific location. Let us now extend it, by using our newly-acquired knowledge of template variables, to also show the resource title. The resource-specific variable for this is pagetitle. Modify the template by adding the highlighted segment, which we have created to contain the title, giving the following HTML:

```
<!DOCTYPE html PUBLIC "-//W3C//DTD XHTML 1.1//EN"
  "http://www.w3.org/TR/xhtml11/DTD/xhtml11.dtd">
<html xmlns="http://www.w3.org/1999/xhtml" xml:lang="en">
<head>
<title>Learning Modx</title>
<meta http-equiv="Content-Type" content="text/html;
charset=iso-8859-1" />
<link rel="stylesheet" type="text/css" href=" assets/templates/
learningMODx/style.css " />
</head>
<body>
<div id="banner">
<h1>Learning MODx</h1>
</div>
<div id="wrapper">
```

```
<div id="container">
  <div id="content">
    [*pagetitle*]
  <br/>
    [*#content*]
  </div>
</div>
<div class="clearing"></div>
</div> <!-- end of wrapper div -->
<div id="footer">It is fun and exciting to build websites with MODx</
div></body>
</html>
```

Changing existing templates

Follow these steps to change the code of an existing template:

1. Click on the **Elements** menu in the top navigation panel.
2. Click on the **Manage Elements** menu item.
3. Click on the template to be edited—in this case, the Learning MODx default template.
4. Replace the existing HTML with the preceding HTML.
5. Click on the **Save** button to store the changes.
6. Click on the **Preview** menu item in the **Site** menu to see the preview.

You will see something like the example shown in the following screenshot:

As you can see, the template now displays the page title (**Home**) before the content.

Template variables

We have already discussed a special type of template variable called resource-specific variables.

In this section, we will cover the creation of template variables that are specific to templates. We will be using the concepts covered here, throughout the book, for practical examples. This section provides you with a theoretical background that eases the understanding when using template variables in the corresponding chapters. To explain template variables, let us consider a blog site. Each blog entry can have some values attached to it, such as a tag and a rating. A **tag** is just a value assigned to a blog page that specifies which category this blog page belongs to, and a **rating** allows the visitors to rate the quality of the blog. All these values, which can be different for each resource, can be stored by using template variables. Hence a template variable is a property of a template that has individual values for each resource using the template. In this section, you will learn the following:

- Creating template variables
- The types of values that a template variable can store
- Different ways that you can allow a user to change the value of a template variable
- Different sources from which template variables can take their value
- Different presentational methods for the value of template variables

Creating template variables

In this section, you will learn how to create template variables and their various properties, in detail. Start creating your template variable by following these steps:

1. Click on the **Elements** menu in the top navigation panel.
2. Click on the **Manage Elements** menu item.
3. Click on the **Template Variables** tab in the rightmost content area.
4. Click on **New Template Variable**.

You will see a screen like the one shown in the following screenshot:

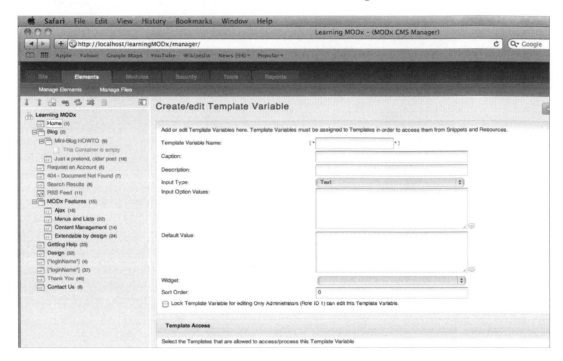

The following is an explanation of the fields, as displayed on the screen. (You don't have to enter anything at this stage.)

- **Template Variable Name** — the name of the template variable that is to be created.

- **Caption** — it is like the title of a template variable that makes it easier for you to remember which template variable does what. It is recommended that you use the same name for **Caption** as the **Template Variable Name**.

- **Description** — a description of the template variable, which will help you to remember its purpose.

- **Input type**, **Input option values** — this is related to the type of value that a variable can store (discussed in the next section).

- **Default Value** — the value that this template variable will hold for every document, unless a different value is assigned.

- **Widget**, **Sort Order** — this is related to the presentation methods for the value of template variables (discussed in the following sections).

- **Template Access** — this allows you to select which templates can make use of this variable.

- **Access Permissions**—this is related to permissions (explained in the next chapter).
- **Category**—this is similar to the category concept for templates, as explained in the section *Creating a new template and giving it a category*. The category is just for your easy identification.

Template variable values

In this section, we will discuss the different kinds of values that a template variable can store. The input type drop-down box allows you to choose the input types for template variables. These will be the input fields that will be added to the document editing page in the Manager. They will appear as new fields below the main Content field in documents. The following are the different data types that a template variable can store:

- Text
- Textarea
- Textarea (Mini)
- RichText
- DropDown List Menu
- Listbox (Single-Select)
- Listbox (Multi-Select)
- Radio Options
- Check Box
- Image
- File
- URL
- Email
- Number
- Date

Data types that allow a user to select from choices must define what those choices are, for example, the drop-down box and listbox values that are defined in the **Input Option Values** field. Each option that is available is separated using the following sequence of characters: ||. For example, if you want the user to select between red and yellow, you would change the **Input Option Values** field to red || yellow. Such sequences of characters that separate different elements in a list are generally called **delimiters**.

You can also provide a default value for any of the data types, in the **Default Value** field.

Data source binding

Data source bindings allow the input option values and the default value to be retrieved from an external source, such as a file or a database. This can be helpful when there are a lot of values, or values that will change over time. The following is a list of keywords that function as a data source when used in the **Input Option Values** or **Default Value** field:

- @FILE—gets the data from the contents of the specified file; for example, @FILE colors.txt.

- @DOCUMENT—gets the data from the contents of the given resource ID; for example, @DOCUMENT 22.

- @CHUNK—gets the data from the contents of the given chunk. Chunks are discussed in the following sections.

- @SELECT—gets the data by querying a database.

- @EVAL—gets the data from the result returned by the given PHP code.

- @INHERIT—gets the data from the given content. If no content is given, it looks for the content of the same variable in the parent document, and continues up to the root document until it finds a value.

- @DIRECTORY—shows the list of files within a specified folder

Widgets

Widgets format the output of the template variable to be displayed on the final web page. So **Input Type** determines what will be displayed when editing the document, and **Widgets** determine how this will be displayed in the final web page output.

The following is a list of the available widgets in MODx:

- Data Grid
- Floater
- Marquee
- RichText
- Ticker
- View Port
- HTML Entities
- Date Formatter
- Unixtime
- Delimited List

- HTML Generic Tag
- Hyperlink
- Image
- String Formatter

Each of these options has configurations attached to it. Certain widget options will be explained in detail, as we use them, in the remaining chapters.

Creating a blog site

Now that we have created a template, we can create any number of resources that can use the same template. Now let us extend this behavior further to allow a user to create a resource by using some interface in the site without having to use the Manager interface. In the next section, you will find the required theory behind what we are going to do. All that we do here is create a resource that shows a form that contains fields relating to a blog post to the end user. When the end user fills in the content and submits the data, a new resource is created.

Using a Snippet

For continuing with the rest of the section, we are going to use a snippet called `NewsEditor`. Previously, this snippet was included with MODx. Later in the book, we further discuss installing and creating your own snippets. For the purpose of this chapter, it is enough to get the snippet installed and functioning by doing the following:

1. Download the Snippet folder from `http://modxcms.com/extras/dl.html?file=506`, and extract it.

2. In the Manager interface, click on the **Manage Elements** menu item in the **Elements** menu.

3. Click on the **Snippets** tab, and then click on the **New Snippet** link.

4. Give the snippet name as **NewsEditor**.

5. Paste the code from the file `NewsEditor.txt` from the downloaded folder into the snippet code area.

6. Make sure that you have copied and pasted the code from the file within `<?php   ?>`, such that the start of the code is after `<?php and ?>`.

You may fill in a description, if you like, and then click on the **Save** button.

Creating a resource

We will now create a resource to show a basic blog form and then process the posted data. Create the new resource by clicking on the **new resource** icon in the left panel.

Populate the following fields, and then save the document:

Field Name	Field
Title	**Post a Blog!**
Long Title	**Post a Blog!**
Description	This page allows a user to post a blog entry
Template	**Learning MODx default template** (should have been selected by default)

You will find the newly-created document and its assigned ID. You will be using this ID in the following steps. It will be referred to as PID.

1. Click on the document, and then click **Edit**.

2. Change the **Editor** of **Document Content** to **none**.

3. Fill the **Document Content** with the following content:

   ```
   [!NewsEditor &folder=`PID` &makefolder=`1`!]
   ```

   Use the back-tick character (`` ` ``) and not a single quote (').

   There should not be any line breaks between [! and !]. In other words, do not click *Enter* in the middle of the statement. Sometimes, when the string is longer, the browser displays it in multiple lines. That is fine, but there should not be line breaks. There should not be any spaces between the [! and the template variable name like [! TVName.

4. Replace PID with the ID of the current document. (The ID is highlighted in the following image.)

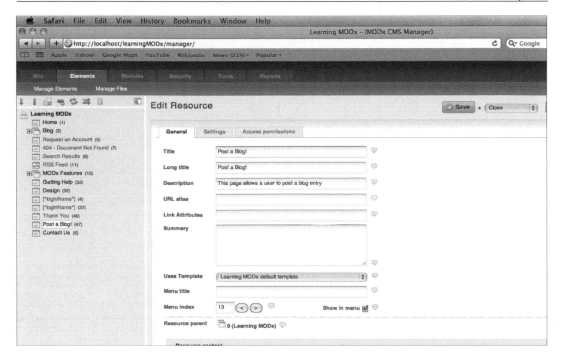

The preceding screenshot shows the ID of the document and that being used as the PID in the snippet call.

7. Save the document.

 It is possible to refer to the current resource by using [*id*].

Blog entry

Now that you have created a mechanism to post a blog entry, let us see how it works. Right-click on the newly-created document, and then click on **Preview**.

You will see a page like the one shown in the following screenshot:

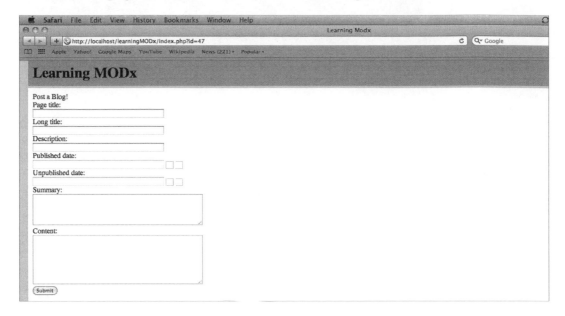

Fill in the fields with the following information, and then click on the **Submit** button:

- **Page title**: **My First Blog**
- **Long title**: **My First Blog in my own site**
- **Description**: **Posting a blog using the Post a Blog! page**
- **Published date**: leave empty
- **Unpublished date**: leave empty
- **Summary**: **Blogging is fun**
- **Content**: **Let's all start blogging**

A new resource is created and displayed.

Now, in the `manager` folder, click on the refresh icon in the left panel, and you will notice that the blog creation page has turned into a folder with a + symbol. If you click on it, you will see that it contains the newly-created resource.

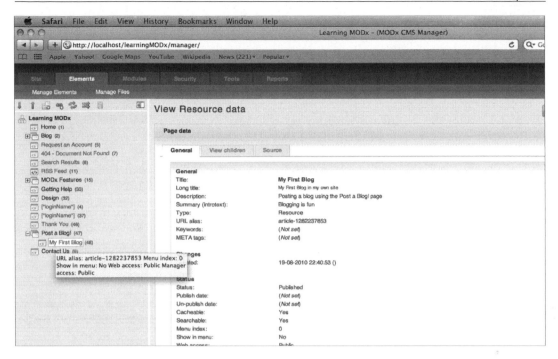

You have now successfully created a basic blog interface and have also posted a blog entry. It is time to understand what is happening and to tweak the interface a bit.

Snippet and chunk basics

Snippets are executable PHP code objects that provides some functionality when called.

In the previous example, `NewsEditor` is a snippet. The only content of the **Post a Blog!** page was the call to the `NewsEditor` snippet; the snippet takes care of displaying a form and storing the values entered through it as a new document. There is a whole chapter on *Snippets* in this book (*Chapter 8, Snippets*). In this section, you will learn the bare minimum about snippets that is necessary to follow along in the ensuing chapters.

Generating output

Most snippets return an output that gets shown in the template at the same location from which the call to the snippet was made.

Such output can be returned by snippets in two ways:

- Return the HTML: In this method, there is less control over what the snippet returns. Changes in the returned output can only be made by editing the snippet code, as the snippet has the HTML that has to be returned within the snippet code.

- Use chunks: Snippets can render output by using chunks that use placeholders in the same way that a template does. The snippet can create these placeholders and store values in them. When a snippet uses chunks to render output, each placeholder that the chunk will be using is created and its value is assigned by the snippet. Then the template renders a chunk by replacing the placeholders in the chunk with their values.

Let us look into the call that we made to the NewsEditor, again.

```
[!NewsEditer? &folder=`PID` &makefolder=`1`!]
```

There are a few things to note here:

- Calls to snippets can be made by enclosing the snippet name within [! and !]

- A snippet can accept parameters that can alter its behavior, such as folder and makefolder in the last example

- Parameters are passed as a key and value pair in the format key=value

- The snippet name and the parameters are separated by the ? symbol, which follows immediately after the snippet name

- Every parameter has an & symbol appended to the key

- The values of parameters are contained within ` symbols

Snippet calls can also be made by enclosing the snippet name within [[ ]]. The difference between [[ ]] and [! !] is that the former is cached and the latter is uncached. **Caching** is a technique that is used to improve performance by saving a processed value to avoid processing it again on further calls. In MODx, resources can be cached. When we use the uncached notation for calling snippets, the snippet will still be processed, in order to ensure that the content of the snippet is always dynamic, even in a cached page. It does not matter in an uncached page as in an uncached page, the snippet is always processed, irrespective of the notation.

NewsEditor is a snippet that displays a form and stores the posted information as a resource. It can be configured to work in many different ways, depending on the parameters passed along. We will discuss this in more detail in the chapter on *Snippets*. The following list explains a few parameters that are of interest in this chapter:

- `folder` — specifies under which container the newly-created resources should be placed
- `makefolder` — if the given value for the parameter above is only a resource and not a container then, the value in this parameter controls whether or not the resource is automatically converted to a container
- `formtpl` — a customized form is shown from a chunk specified by this parameter
- `rtcontent` — when this is specified, the given field will be treated as rich text instead of raw text
- `Template` — the resource that is created by `NewsEditor` will use the template mentioned here

Having created a simple blog interface, we are going to make two enhancements by using what we have learned, which will be explained in the following sections.

Using a custom form for the Post a Blog! page

To customize the form, all that we need to do is create a form in HTML, save it as a chunk, and then pass the name of this chunk as the value of `formtpl` to `NewsEditor`.

We need a mechanism by which we can let the `NewsEditor` snippet know which text field, from the resource, gets stored as which property. For example, we might have a title, summary, and content, and we will want the title to be saved as the resource-specific variable `longtitle`, the summary as the resource-specific variable `description`, and the content field as the content of the resource. This has to be explicitly specified, as `NewsEditor` has no ability to make guesses about which field gets stored as what in the resource.

When using a chunk as a form template along with `NewsEditor`, the specification of what field gets stored as what variable in the resource is done by setting the name attribute of the form element to the resource-specific variable. The following is the HTML for the custom blog form. There are more concepts to discuss on snippets like `NewsEditor` and how to use chunks with them. These are dealt with in the later chapters.

HTML for the custom blog form

The following is the code for the chunk that will be used by the `NewsEditor` snippet, in order to render a custom form:

```
<div id="blogpage">
<form action="[~[*id*]~]" method="post" name="NewsEditor">
  <table>
    <h3> Blog Entry </h3>
    <br />
    <input name="NewsEditorForm" type="hidden" value="on" />
  </table>
  <table>
    <tbody>
      <tr>
        <td><label for="pagetitle">Title</label></td>
        <td> <input id="pagetitle" name="pagetitle" size="40"
                type="text" value="[+pagetitle+]" /></td>
      </tr>
      <tr>
        <td><label for="introtext">Summary </label></td>
        <td><textarea cols="50" name="introtext"
                rows="5">[+introtext+]</textarea></td>
      </tr>
      <tr>
        <td><label for="content">Content</label></td>
        <td> <textarea cols="50" name="content"
                rows="5">[+content+]</textarea></td>
      </tr>
    </tbody>
  </table>
  <input class="button" name="send" type="submit" value="Blog it!" />
</form>
</div>
```

Steps to create a chunk

Now that we have the HTML ready for the chunk, we will create the chunk in this section.

1. Click on the **Manage Elements** menu item in the **Elements** menu.

2. Click on the **Chunks** tab, and then click on **New Chunk**.

3. Fill in the following data in the new chunk page:

Field Name	Value
Chunk name	**blogform**
Description	**Form template for posting a blog**
Existing Category	**Learning MODx**
Chunk code	The HTML above
Editor to use	None

4. Click on the **Save** button.

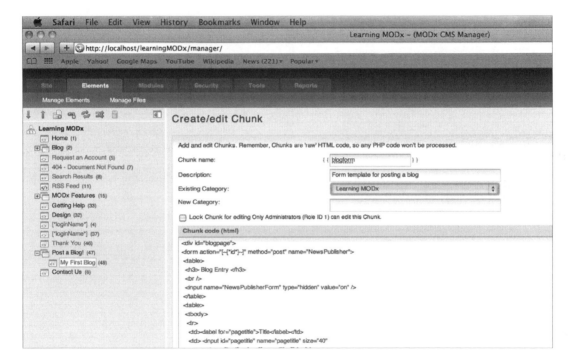

Using a chunk as a form template

The following are the steps necessary to make `NewsEditor` use the created chunk as the form template:

1. Click on the **Post a Blog!** resource, and then click on **Edit**.

2. Replace the document content with the following:

```
[!NewsEditor? &folder=`47` &makefolder=`1` &formtpl=`blogform`
                    &template=`Learning MODx blog`!]
```

Note that you will have to replace 47 with the ID of the resource **Post a Blog!** and make sure that the entire snippet call is, as mentioned earlier, in a single line without a line break. It is alright if the browser displays it as two lines, but there should not be a line break in the code.

3. Click on the **Save** button.

Also, as you can guess from the snippet call, we are creating a new template for all blogs. For now, this template will be the same as the Learning MODx default template. To create the template, carry out the steps shown below:

1. Open the Learning MODx blog template from **Templates** in the **Manage Elements** submenu.

2. Click on **Duplicate**, and click **Ok** when asked.

3. Change the template name to **Learning MODx blog template**.

4. Select the **Category** as **Learning MODx**.

5. Click on **Save.**

Checking the Post a Blog! page

Now that we are using a custom form template, let us check to see if it works.

1. Right-click on the **Post a Blog!** page, and then click on **Preview**.

2. Fill in the fields with the following content, and then click on the **Blog it!** button:

Field Name	Value
Title	**My Second Blog Entry**
Summary	**Just created a custom blog template**
Content	**It is simple and quick to allow well written snippets to take advantage of custom formatting using chunks**

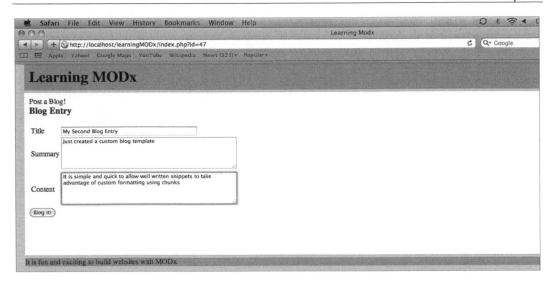

You will see the posted blog entry on a new page:

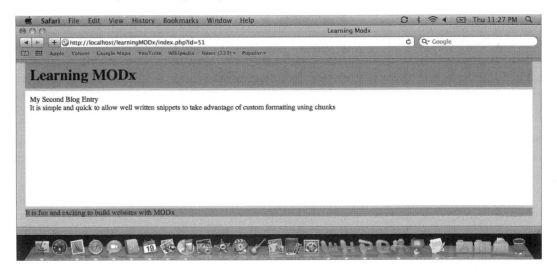

Rich text editor for the blog content

To provide a rich text editor for the blog content area, all that has to be done is to replace the content area with a template variable that is of the rich text type and uses the rich text widget. This way, MODx provides a rich-text editor automatically when the form is being filled in or edited. This is a three-step process:

- Creation of the template variable
- Making the form template chunk use the template variable
- Letting NewsEditor be aware that the content field has changed to the new template variable

Creating the template variable

1. Click on the **Manage Elements** menu item in the **Elements** menu.
2. Click on the **Template Variables** tab, and then click on **New Template Variable**.
3. Fill in the fields with the following values:

Field Name	Value
Template Variable Name	**blogRT**
Description	**Template Variable to store rich text for the blogs**
Input Type	**Rich Text**
Widget	**Rich Text**
Widget width	**100%**
Widget height	**300px**
Editor	**TinyMCE**
Template Access	**Learning MODx default template**
Existing Category	**Learning MODx**

4. Click on **Save**.

Chunk and template variable

Now that we have created a template variable with the rich text widget, let us modify the form template to use it.

The HTML of the blogform chunk has to be replaced with the following:

```
<div id="blogpage">
<form action="[~[*id*]~]" method="post" name="NewsEditor">
  <table>
```

```
   <h3> Blog Entry </h3>
   <br />
   <input name="NewsEditorForm" type="hidden" value="on" />
</table>
<table>
<tbody>
  <tr>
    <td><label for="pagetitle">Title</label></td>
    <td> <input id="pagetitle" name="pagetitle" size="40"
              type="text" value="[+pagetitle+]" /></td>
  </tr>
  <tr>
    <td><label for="introtext">Summary </label></td>
    <td><textarea cols="50" name="introtext"
    rows="5">[+introtext+]</textarea></td>
  </tr>
  <tr>
    <td><label for="content">Content</label></td>
    <td> [*blogRT*]</td>
  </tr>
</tbody>
</table>
<input class="button" name="send" type="submit" value="Blog it!" />
</form>
</div>
```

Instead of calling a form field, such as `textarea`, with the name of the resource-specific variable, we have replaced that line with a call to the template variable (see the highlighted line in the previous code). This single line performs all of the necessary functionalities to make the template variable editable, by using the selected widget according to the content type.

To replace the previous HTML in the form template chunk, do the following:

1. Click on the **Manage Elements** menu item in the **Elements** menu.
2. Click on the **Chunks** tab.
3. Click on the **blogform** chunk.
4. Replace the HTML in the **Chunk Code** area with the previous HTML.
5. Click on **Save**.

Now, right-click on the **Post a Blog!** page, click **Preview**, and you will see something like the example shown in the following screenshot:

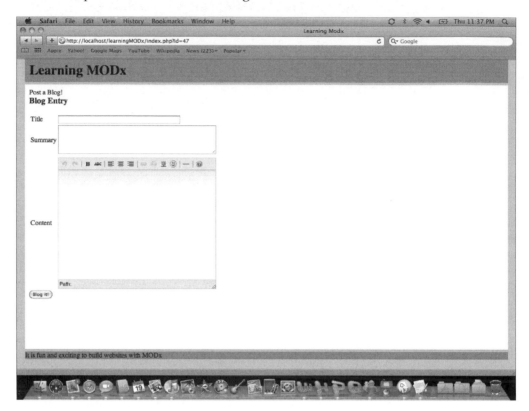

NewsEditor and the Rtcontent field

You have now enabled the content field to use the rich text editor. However, NewsEditor is still expecting the blog content to come from a form field with the name **Content**. Hence, when it is saving the form, it will throw a validation error stating that the news content is missing. When you try to post a blog entry now, the following is the error that you will get:

We can correct this by passing the value of the new template variable by using the `rtcontent` parameter.

To do that, edit the **Post a Blog!** page, as mentioned in the previous sections, and replace the code with the following:

```
[!NewsEditor? &folder=`47` &makefolder=`1` &formtpl=`blogform`
&template=`Learning MODx blog` &rtcontent=`tvblogRT` !]
```

Save the document and preview it.

Now, you will be able to use the rich text editor for the content area and post blogs. Go ahead and post a few blogs to check if it works.

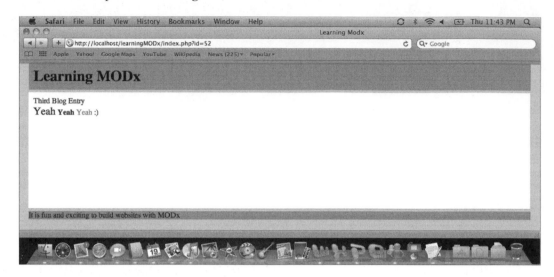

Summary

In this chapter, you have learned about:

- Templates
  - ○ Creation/addition
  - ○ Flow of rendering

- Template variables and resource specific variables
  - ○ Data types
  - ○ Widgets
  - ○ Data sources

- Snippets and chunks

You have also, during the process, created:

- A template for the site
- A snippet from the web
- Blog functionality
- Custom form template for the blog page
- A rich text editor for the blog

5
Authentication and Authorization

Authentication is the process of verifying that users are who they claim to be. **Authorization** is the process of granting access to authenticated users—based on their role—to perform operations such as view, edit, or delete for resources. In this chapter, you will learn how MODx facilitates authentication and authorization. You will build your site to include user registrations, logins, and user types, and will also set rules on who can do what.

As you read this chapter, it is important that you keep in mind that MODx has two user types:

- Web Users—users who use the website
- Manager Users—users who are allowed to log in to the Manager interface

It is vital to keep this distinction in mind in order to be able to understand the complexities explained in this chapter.

You will also learn in this chapter how MODx allows the grouping of resources, users, and permissions.

Creating a web user

Let us start by creating a web user. Web users are users who can access restricted resource groups in the website (frontend); they do not have Manager access.

Web users can identify themselves at login by using login forms. They are allowed to log in from the user page, but they cannot log in using the Manager interface. To create a web user, perform the following steps:

1. Click on the **Web Users** menu item in the **Security** menu.
2. Click on **New Web User**.
3. Fill in the fields with the following information:

Field Name	Value
Username	samira
Password	samira123
Email Address	xyz@configurelater.com

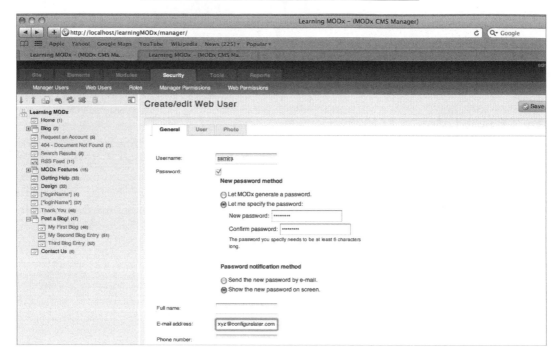

4. Click on the **Save** button.

Now you will see a page like the example shown in the following screenshot, which lists all of the web users on your site:

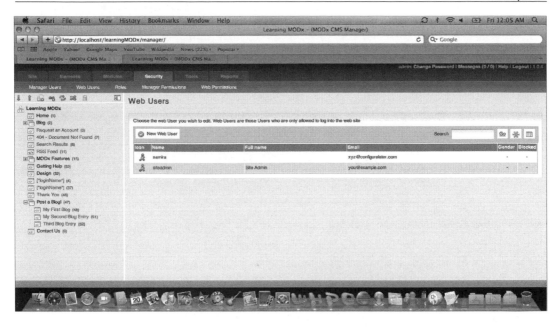

Other user properties

When you click on any user on the web users' page, a page opens that allows you to edit the existing information and also shows simple statistics, such as when the user last logged in. It is also possible to block or unblock the particular user from this page. You can also set **Blocked Until** or **Blocked After** to block a user for a certain period and to schedule such a block. When a user is blocked, MODx does not allow that user to log in.

There is also a **Photo** tab, where you can upload a picture for a user.

In the **User** tab, you have the following fields:

- **Login Home Page**: Here you can specify the document that the user is shown immediately after login.

- **Allowed IP Address**: It is possible to allow certain users to log in only from specific machines. This can be set for a particular user by specifying the IP address of the machines in this field, separated by a comma.

- **Allowed Days**: It is possible to allow certain users to log in only on certain days of the week. This can be set for the particular user by selecting which days the user is allowed to log in.

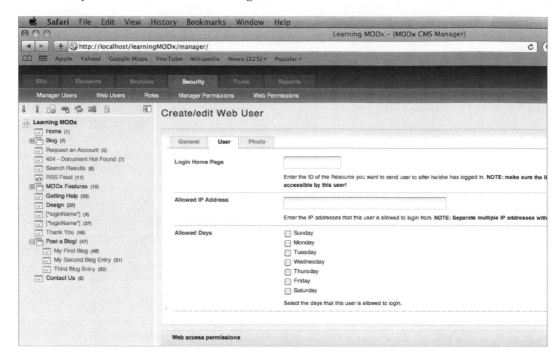

Add the login snippet

Now that we have created a user, let us add a login form that allows the user to log in to the site.

This process is very simple. All that you have to do is call the WebLogin snippet in the template where you want the login page to be shown. We are going to change the template HTML with the following HTML for the Learning MODx default template:

```
<!DOCTYPE html PUBLIC "-//W3C//DTD XHTML 1.1//EN" "http://www.w3.org/
TR/xhtml11/DTD/xhtml11.dtd"> <html xmlns="http://www.w3.org/1999/
xhtml" xml:lang="en">
<head>
  <base href="[(site_url)]"></base>
  <title>Learning MODx</title>
  <meta http-equiv="Content-Type" content="text/html; charset=iso-
                                              8859-1" />
  <link rel="stylesheet" type="text/css" href="assets/templates/
learningMODx/style.css" />
```

```
    </head>
    <body>
      <div id="banner">
       <h1>Learning MODx</h1>
      </div>
      <div id="wrapper">
        <div id="container">
          <div id="content">
            <div id="col-1">
              <h1>[*pagetitle*]</h1>
              <br/>
              [*#content*]
            </div>
            <div id="col-2" >
            <div > [!WebLogin!] </div>
            </div>
          </div>
        </div>
        <div class="clearing"> </div>
      </div> <!-- end of wrapper div -->
      <div id="footer">It is fun and exciting to build websites with
            MODx</div>
    </body>
    </html>
```

Notice that the only addition is the call to the [!WebLogin!] snippet besides the
change in the HTML layout, which now has two div elements id=col-1 and
id=col-2, within the div that has id=content , in order to split the content area into
two panes.

Also, because we have made changes to the layout, we will have to change the
style.css file to specify the width of col-1 and col-2. The new style.css
should be changed to:

```
* { padding:2; margin:0; border:1; }
body { margin:0 20px; background:#8CEC81; }
#banner { background: #2BB81B; border-top:5px solid #8CEC81; border-
            bottom:5px solid #8CEC81; }
#banner h1 { padding:10px; }
#wrapper { background: #8CEC81; }
#container { width: 100%; background: #2BB81B; float: left; }
#content { background: #ffffff; height:600px; padding:0 10px 10px
            10px; clear:both; }
#footer { background: #2BB81B; border-top:5px solid #8CEC81; border-
            bottom:5px solid #8CEC81; }
.clearing { clear:both; height:0; }
```

```
#content #col-1 {float:left;width:500px; margin:0px;padding:0px;}
#content #col-2 {float:right; width:300px; margin:0px; padding:30px 0
          10px 25px; border-left:3px solid #99cc66; height:500px;}
#content #col-2 div {padding-bottom:20px;}
```

The following are the steps to change the template to use a login snippet and to style it as described above:

1. Click on the **Manage Elements** menu item of the **Elements** menu.
2. Click on the **Learning MODx** default template.
3. Replace it with the preceding HTML.
4. Click on the **Save** button.
5. Open the `style.css` file that you created earlier, from the `learningMODx` folder.
6. Replace it with the preceding style code and then save the file.

Now preview the Home Page; it should look similar to the example shown in the following screenshot:

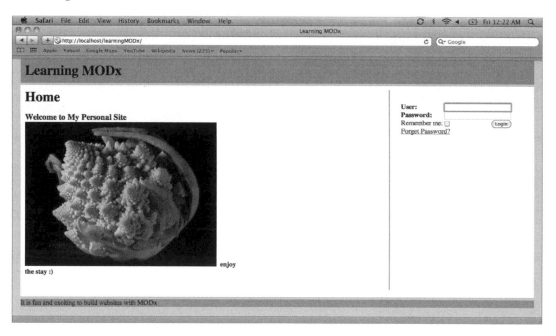

Log in as **samira**. The screen will now look something like the following:

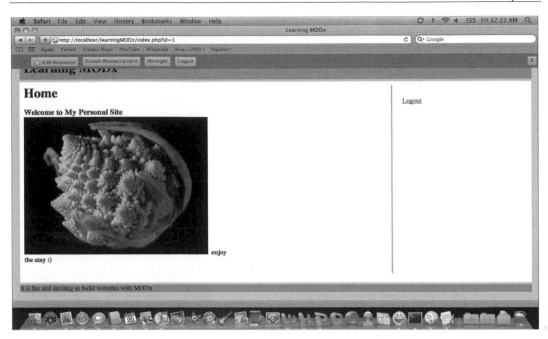

Notice that the **Doc Manager** bar is dependent on whom you log in as from the Manager interface, and not on whom you log in as from the Web interface. You can check this out by clicking on the **Logout** link on the Manager page and refreshing the Home Page. The **Doc Manager** bar does not appear.

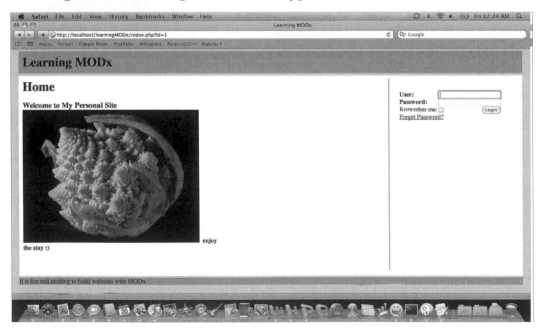

Resources can be assigned to resource groups, and permissions can be defined on resource groups. In our site, we want only our friends to post a blog, although anyone can write a comment. So we will create a user group called **Friends**, and assign all of the friends that we want to allow to blog to this group.

Perform the following steps to create the **Friends** user group:

1. Click on the **Web Permissions** menu item on the **Security** menu.

2. Click on the **Web User groups** tab if it is not already selected.

3. In the **Create a new user group** box, type **Friends**.

4. Click on the **Submit** button.

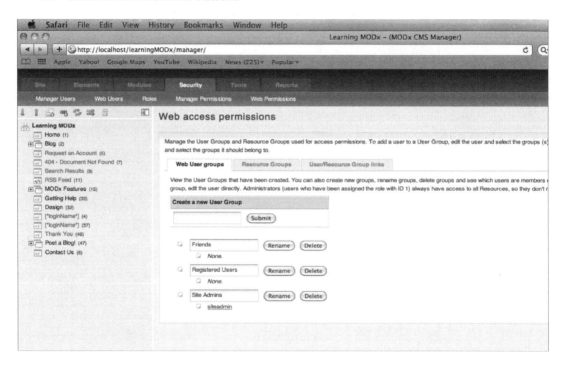

Resource group for friends

Now that we have a user group called **Friends**, we need to specify which otherwise-inaccessible resources are accessible to this group. We can group all of these resources into a resource group. The following are the steps to create a resource group:

1. Click on the **Web Permissions** menu item on the **Security** menu.

2. Click on the **Resource groups** tab if it is not already selected.

3. In the **Create a new Resource group** box, type **onlyforfriends**.

4. Click on the **Submit** button.

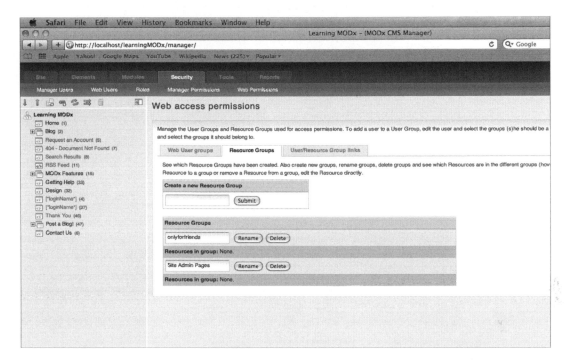

Restricting access for a resource

All of the resources so far have been created as **All Resource Groups (Public)**. This means that anybody can access the resources. When we assign a resource to some other group, then only the users belonging to that particular group can access it. Now let us change the resource group of **Post a Blog** to **onlyforfriends** as follows:

1. Click on the **Post a Blog!** resource from the document tree.
2. Click on the **Edit** button.
3. Click on the **Access Permissions** tab.
4. Enable the **onlyforfriends** checkbox.
5. Click on the **Save** button.

User group: Resource group

If you have logged in as **samira** from the website, log off and preview the **Post a Blog!** page. You will still see the blog page. This is because when we assign a resource to a resource group, it is still accessible to everyone. Only when a user group is linked to a document group do the permissions become exclusive to that group. Now let us link the **Friends** user group to the **onlyforfriends** resource group.

1. Click on the **Web Permissions** menu item of the **Security** menu.

2. Click on **User/Resource group links**.

3. Select the **onlyforfriends** group from the drop-down box next to the **Friends** user group, and then click on the **Submit** button.

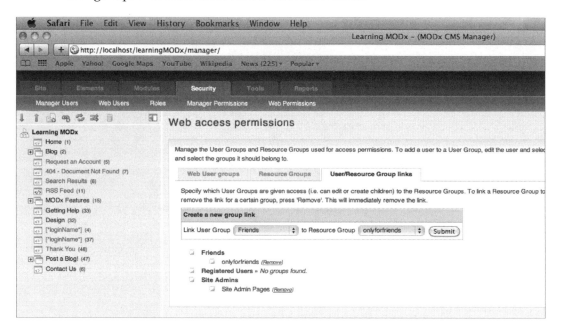

User: User group

Now preview the **Post a Blog!** page again, and you will see something like the example shown in the following screenshot:

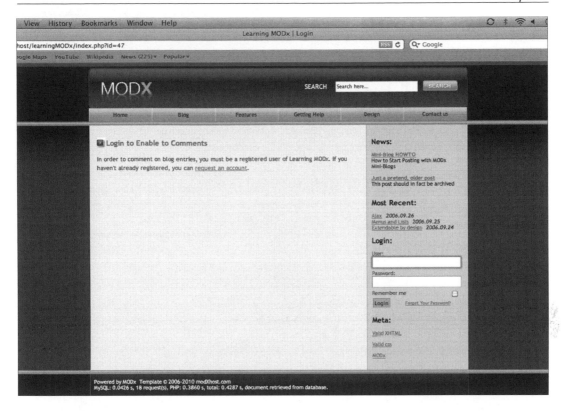

Forget about the inappropriate message for now; we will deal with that at the end of the chapter. What you must understand now is that MODx has denied access to this page, and has redirected the user to the permission denied page that was initially set in the site configuration.

Try logging in as **samira** from the home page and visiting the **Post a Blog!** page again. You are still unauthorized to view the page. The user **samira** can only access the **Post a Blog!** page if **samira** is a member of the **Friends** user group. This is because we mapped the **Friends** user group to the **onlyforfriends** resource group, and **Post a Blog!** belongs to the **onlyforfriends** resource group. So let us go ahead and add **samira** to the **Friends** user group.

1. Click on the **Web Users** menu item of the **Security** menu.
2. Click on the username **samira**.
3. Click on the **General** tab, if it was not selected already.
4. Select the **Friends** checkbox in the **Web access permissions** section.
5. Click on the **Save** button.

Now, having logged in as **samira** from the home page, visit the **Post a Blog!** page. You should be able to see the regular blog page.

Post moderation

It will be helpful if we can delegate the role of moderating blogs to someone else. The user must only be able to manipulate the resources (**Edit or Delete**) from the Manager interface, and should not be able to perform any other activity. There are two points to note here:

- Able to manipulate resources from the Manager interface — must be a Manager user type
- Not able to perform any other activity — create a custom role only for manipulating resources

Creating a role

Let us create a role called **Blog Moderators** who can only edit resources.

1. Click on the **Roles** menu item of the **Security** menu.
2. Click on **Create/edit role** and fill in the following information:

Field Name	Field Value
Role name	Blog Moderators
Description	Role type that allows only administration of documents

3. Enable the following checkboxes in **Content management**:
   - ° **Edit a Resource**
   - ° **Delete Resources**
4. Click on the **Save** button.

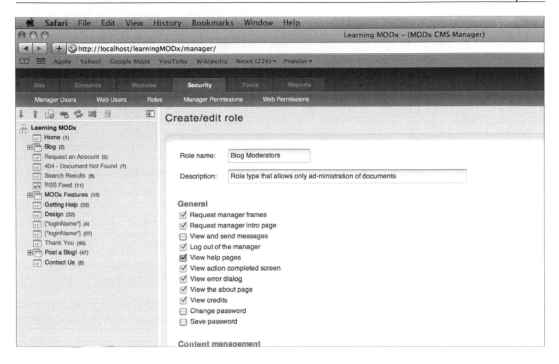

Creating a Manager user

Let us create a Manager user called **blogmoderator1**, who will moderate all of the blogs:

1. Click on the **Manager Users** menu item in the **Security** menu.

2. Click on **New User** and fill in the following information:

Field Name	Field Value
Username	**blogmoderator1**
Password	**blogmoderator1**
Email	**asd@configurelater.com**
Role	**Blog Moderators**

3. Click on the **Save** button.

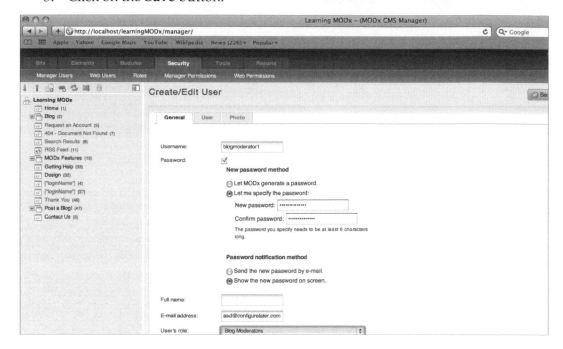

Checking the new role

Now that you have created a new role and have assigned a user to that role, let us try to log in as that user. First, log out from the Manager interface and log in again with the username **blogmoderator1** and password **blogmoderator1**. You will see a screen like the one shown in the following screenshot:

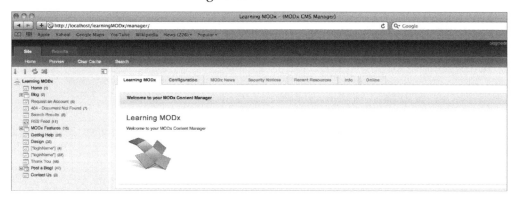

As you can see, you have been able to log in to the Manager interface successfully. You will also notice that you are allowed to do only the activities that were enabled for this user. You may want to sign back in as the admin for the rest of the book.

User registration

We have already seen how new users can be created. In addition to creating users from the Manager interface, users can also be allowed to register from a Web interface. Such users can also be assigned to a default user group.

Showing a signup form

To show a signup form, we will use a snippet (WebSignup) that comes bundled with MODx.

1. Create a new resource, and fill in the following information:

Field Name	Value
Title	**Signup Form**
Uses Template	**Learning MODx default template**
Resource Content	**[!WebSignup!]**

2. Click on the **Save** button.

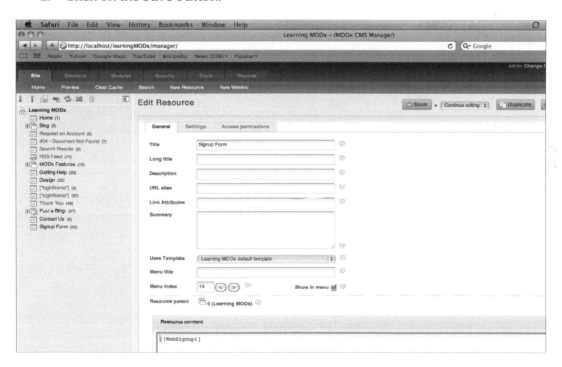

Notice that the content of the document is only [!WebSignup!], which is a call to the snippet WebSignup, which displays a user registration form.

Now preview the page and it will look like the example shown in the following screenshot:

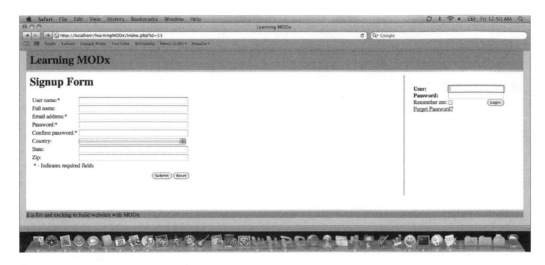

Joining a default group

To assign registering users to the **Friends** user group, change the **Resource Content** field on the sign up form that we have just created to the following:

```
[!WebSignup? &groups=`Friends`!]
```

Notice that this functionality allows WebSignup to be called multiple times, with different parameters, in order to have separate login forms for different kinds of users. You can even have different forms by setting a template parameter for the rendered forms.

Link the signup form in the log in snippet

Now that we have created a User Registration page, we need to add a link to this page. Add the following code at the end of the resource home page:

```
<br/><a href="[~57~]">Register</a>
```

Note: Replace 57 with the appropriate resource id of the signup page.

We are just creating a link to the signup page in our home page.

Now the home Page will appear like the example shown in the following screenshot:

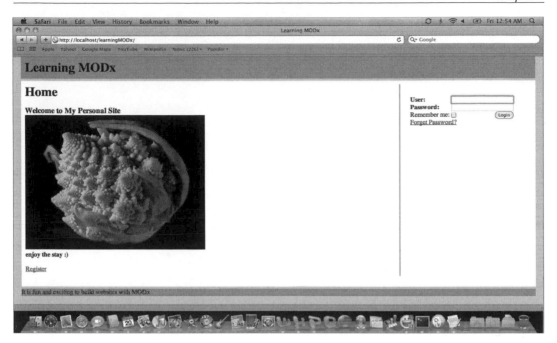

Snippets and authorization

So far, we have seen authentication and authorization with regard to:

- Web users and resources
- Managers and roles

Authorization on a resource level restricts access or grants permission to a user for the entire resource. Authorization within snippets can make this more granular by restricting only certain content within a resource that is being rendered by the snippet. As explained in the previous chapter, snippets accept parameters, and certain snippets provide parameters to be configured so that they are accessible only by a certain user type. In this section, we will modify the NewsEditor snippet to only allow posts from authenticated users.

NewsPublisher and authentication

In our application we have already restricted access to the **Post a Blog!** page. However, if this was not the case we could have simply edited the contents of the **Post a Blog!** page to the following:

```
[!NewsEditor? &folder=`[*id]` &makefolder=`1` &formtpl=`blogform`
&template=`Learning MODx blog` &rtcontent=`tvblogRT`
&canpost=`Friends` !]
```

This would have configured the snippet to allow access only from the **friends** group.

Summary

We learned about the different types of MODx users. We learned about User groups and resource groups.

We build a signup form and login form and used it to understand authentication and authorization using roles.

There are two categories of MODx users:

- Manager
- Web

We learned that:

- Users can be grouped into User groups
- Resources can be assigned to Resource groups
- Linking Resource groups to Web User groups will control the viewing of resources
- Linking Resource groups to Manager User groups will control manager access to the resources
- Roles define what the manager can do with the accessible resources

We have modified the site to include a signup form and a login form. We have also changed the authorization so that only our friends can post a blog entry.

6

Content Aggregation

In the previous chapters, we have created resources, grouped them in folders, and shown them within templates. Now let us look further into showing short extracts from our content, based on various criteria, such as the most recent or the most viewed resources. This is generally known as content aggregation. Content aggregation extends beyond just displaying extracts from the resources in a web page, and makes it possible to make the content updates available to other applications or to other websites. In this chapter, as we build the site, we will look in detail at the following:

- Aggregation concepts
- MODx's features for aggregation

Ditto

Content aggregation is implemented in MODx by using the snippet **Ditto**. Ditto is so useful and flexible that MODx has a separate site with documentation for this particular core snippet, maintained by Mark Kaplan, the author of Ditto. This chapter discusses in detail the various parameters of this snippet. Ditto is just another snippet, so you can call it from any template or resource in the same way that you call any other snippet. Like any other snippet, its functionality is flexible and configurable by passing appropriate values as parameters. There is also the flexibility to customize the returned results by using placeholders.

Let's start playing with Ditto by creating a resource with the title **Getting to know ditto**, with the content of the resource as:

```
[!Ditto!]
```

Save this resource and preview the page. Now, if you click **Preview**, you will see something like the following:

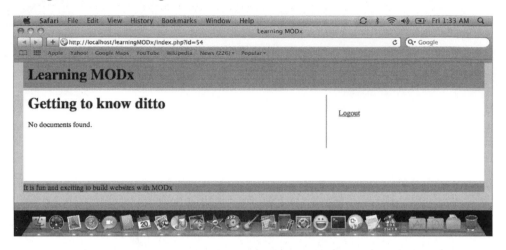

More flexibility with parameters

The preceding screenshot conveys that Ditto has not found any resources. (In the early versions of MODx, resources were called documents, and some snippets still refer to resources as documents). Of course it has not, as we have not specified where to look for the resources. When we do not specify where to look for the resources, Ditto searches by default within the current resource. The current resource from which Ditto was called is not a container that has other resources. There are two parameters that are used to tell Ditto which resource's contents must be aggregated:

- **Parents**: List of parent resources; the children of the parents will be aggregated
- **Documents**: List of individual resources to be aggregated

You can specify a list of resources that must be aggregated by using the `documents` parameter, or you can specify a list of container resources by using the `parents` parameter. When you specify a list of container resources, all of the child resources of the containers will be aggregated.

Let us now modify the resource created in the previous section to use the Post a Blog! container as the parent from which all of the resources must be aggregated.

```
[!Ditto? &parents=`47`!]
```

Replace 47 with the document ID of your Post a Blog! document. Now click on **Preview** and you will see something like this:

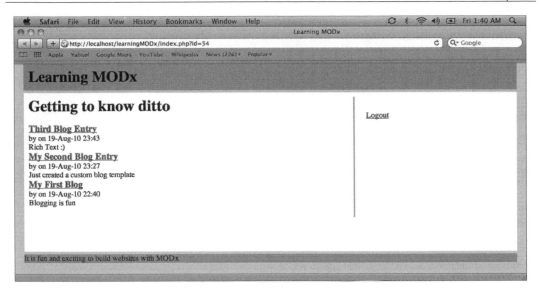

As you can see, all of the resources from the container Post a Blog! are displayed, with the most recently posted resource first. Of course, the sorting order can be changed by passing the appropriate values in the corresponding parameters.

Aggregated data in a template

Now that we have created a resource that aggregates data, let us make the last five blogs appear on every page. We can do this by introducing the Ditto call from within the Learning MODx default template. The call to Ditto would look like this:

```
[!Ditto? &parents=`47` &total=5!]
```

To make the changes, replace the contents of the Learning MODx default template with the following:

```
<!DOCTYPE html PUBLIC "-//W3C//DTD XHTML 1.1//EN" "http://www.w3.org/
TR/xhtml11/DTD/xhtml11.dtd"> <html xmlns="http://www.w3.org/1999/
xhtml" xml:lang="en">
 <head>
  <base href="[(site_url)]"></base>
  <title>Learning MODx</title>
  <meta http-equiv="Content-Type"
        content="text/html; charset=iso-8859-1" />
  <link rel="stylesheet"
        type="text/css"
        href="assets/templates/learningMODx/style.css" />
 </head>
 <body>
```

```
<div id="banner">
 <h1>Learning MODx</h1>
</div>
<div id="wrapper">
 <div id="container">
  <div id="content">
   <div id="col-1">
    <h1>[*pagetitle*]</h1>
    <br/>
    [*#content*]
   </div>
   <div id="col-2" >
    <div > [!WebLogin!] </div>
     <div>
       [!Ditto? &parents=`47` &total=5!]
     </div>
   </div>
  </div>
 </div>
 <div class="clearing"> </div>
</div> <!-- end of wrapper div -->
<div id="footer">It is fun and exciting to build websites with
                                  MODx</div></body>
</html>
```

Click on **Preview**, and you will see something like the following:

Theming MODx—chunks and placeholders

Ditto, like any other snippet, allows theming using placeholders. That is, instead of the snippet returning the complete HTML for each extract of a resource, the snippet returns variables such as content, title, date created, author, and so on, which can be used in a custom chunk. Hence, the chunk will be called for every resource that Ditto is aggregating. Whatever HTML the chunk gets processed into will be the output for that resource.

Let us consider a chunk code like the following:

```
<h3><a href="[~[+id+]~]">[+title+]</a></h3>
[+introtext+]
```

The previous chunk shows the title of the document, along with a link and the summary.

Suppose there are three resources that are aggregated by a particular Ditto call. If that call to Ditto has a parameter that mentions that the preceding chunk should be used as the template, then the chunk will be processed three times, once for each resource. The appropriate title and author name would be inserted for each iteration.

The following is a list of some of the most commonly-used Ditto placeholders.

- [+title+] —shows the title of the resource
- [+summary+] —shows the summary, if it is not empty, or shows an extract from the resource content
- [+link+] —creates a **Read More...** link to the resource
- [+author+] —shows the name of the author in the **Created by** field
- [+id+] —shows the ID of the resource

Now, let us go ahead and theme the aggregation that we have created:

1. Create a chunk with the following data:

Field Name	Value
Title	dittofrontpage
Chunk Code	`<h3><a href="[~[+id+]~]">[+title+]</a></h3>` `[+introtext+]`

2. Change the Learning MODx default template to the following:

```
<!DOCTYPE html PUBLIC "-//W3C//DTD XHTML 1.1//EN" "http://www.
w3.org/TR/xhtml11/DTD/xhtml11.dtd"> <html xmlns="http://www.
w3.org/1999/xhtml" xml:lang="en">
  <head>
```

```
<base href="[(site_url)]"></base>
<title>Learning MODx</title>
<meta http-equiv="Content-Type"
      content="text/html;
      charset=iso-8859-1" />
<link rel="stylesheet"
      type="text/css"
      href="assets/templates/learningMODx/style.css" />
</head>
<body>
 <div id="banner">
  <h1>Learning MODx</h1>
 </div>
 <div id="wrapper">
  <div id="container">
   <div id="content">
    <div id="col-1">
     <h1>[*pagetitle*]</h1>
     <br/>
     [*#content*]
    </div>
    <div id="col-2" >
     <div > [!WebLogin!] </div>
      <div>
        [!Ditto? &parents=`47` &tpl=`dittofrontpage`!]
      </div>
    </div>
   </div>
  </div>
  <div class="clearing"> </div>
 </div> <!-- end of wrapper div -->
 <div id="footer">It is fun and exciting to build websites with
                                    MODx</div></body>
</html>
```

If you refresh the page you will notice that the aggregated content looks different, just as we expected.

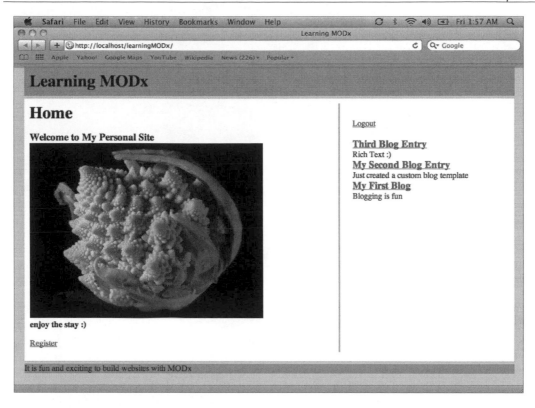

Introducing tagging

Let us use what we have learned so far to allow resources to be tagged for separate categories. For this, we will be:

1. Creating a template variable that will hold the category of a resource.

2. Assigning the resources to a category.

3. Creating separate resources with a Ditto call, in order to show the most recent documents in each category.

Creating a template variable to hold the category

If we want resources to be tagged, the resources must have a field that can hold the category to which they belong. Let's create a template variable that allows you to choose from a list of categories , and give this category the following details:

Field Name	Value
Template Variable Name	blogCategories
Caption	Category
Input Type	Listbox(Multiple-Select)
Input Option Values	Sports | | LifeStyle | | IT
Template Access	Learning MODx blog
Access permissions	onlyforfriends
Existing Category	Learning MODx

Assigning resources to a category

Now that you have created a category, let's go and change the categories of a few resources:

1 Select the resource, and then click **Edit**.
2. Select the category from the drop-down box in the template variable section.
3. Click on **Save**.

Repeat the preceding steps for all of the blog pages that you have created. Now that we have created tags, we can explore how to use them. However, before that, we will have a quick look at the XML formats.

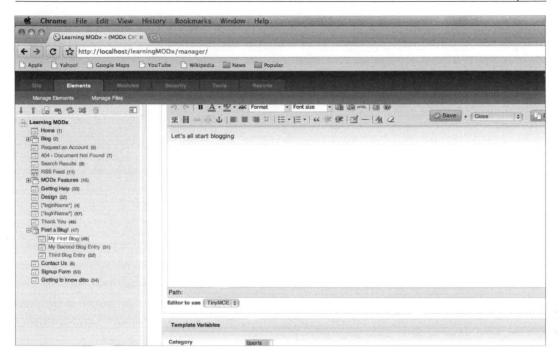

XML formats

It is really interesting that we can have three resources that aggregate and display the blogs belonging to one of the three categories that we have defined. This alone can be useful for showing the recent posts of a site from each category. However, this can be extended further to be more useful, by allowing these resources to render the content in a way that machines understand. We want the content to be processed and displayed by other websites or to be read by the news feed readers.

Machine-readable formats and readers

XML is about generating document definition tags on the fly and placing the data within such tags. Unlike HTML, there is no fixed set of such tags. Hence, to make sense of such tags, the machine reading them must have some prior knowledge of what those tags mean. Groups of such definitions in a specific order and convention are called **Formats**. We have many such formats that are commonly used for sharing data. We also have what are called **Readers**. Readers are websites or applications that process the content in a known format and present it to the user in a usable format. A common example of such a reader is the Google news reader or Gnus mode in Emacs.

Readers

A typical reader asks for a **Feed**. A feed is a URL from which the reader can fetch the data. A reader would consist of different links or buttons for each feed, which, when clicked on, would show the titles of the documents. The users can read the document they wish to, by clicking on its title.

There are various formats that most readers understand. Following is a brief description of them.

- **Really Simple Syndication (RSS)**: This is the most commonly-used format for reading news. Each document represents an article. An article has a title, description, link, and contents.

- **Atom**: This is the same as RSS, but fixes many limitations of RSS. Also, this format can keep track of article updates by registering the timestamps of the modifications.

- **JSON**: This format is widely-used for cross-machine communication. It is widely used when there has to be an exchange of data between applications, even when they are written on two completely different platforms or in different languages.

- **Custom XML**: You can have your own XML format and not use any defined methods.

Ditto and XML formats

To allow Ditto to present the aggregated data as XML, you must keep the following points in mind:

- The resource must be created with the content type as **text/xml**. This can be changed under the **Settings** tab of the resource edit page.

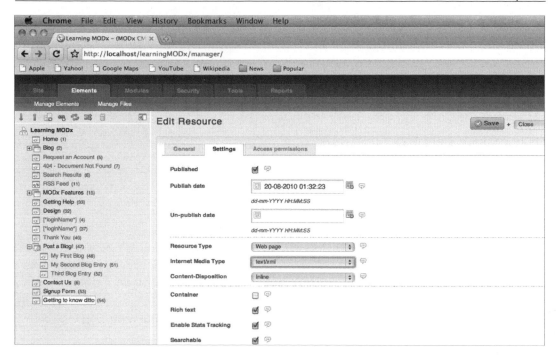

- The template must be selected as blank
- The content must be a call to Ditto, and must have an &format parameter that has a value of one of the following:
    ◦ HTML
    ◦ JSON
    ◦ XML
    ◦ Atom
    ◦ RSS

Creating RSS views for each category

Now that we have categories and understand about aggregation and XML formats, let's create three resources that will display the latest blogs added from a single category. Create three resources with the following details:

Document 1:

Field Name	Value
Title	**Sports RSS**
Use Template	**(Blank)**
Content	`[!Ditto? &parents=`47` &filter=`tvblogCategories,Sports,7` &format=`rss`!]`
Content Type	**text/xml**
Resource Parent	**58** (The ID of your document—Getting to know ditto)

Document 2:

Field Name	Value
Title	**Lifestyle RSS**
Use Template	**(Blank)**
Content	`[!Ditto? &parents=`47` &filter=`tvblogCategories,Lifestyle,7` &format=`rss`!]`
Content Type	**text/xml**
Parent	**58** (The ID of your document—Getting to know ditto)

Document 3:

Field Name	Value
Title	**IT RSS**
Use Template	**(Blank)**
Content	`[!Ditto? &parents=`47` &filter=`tvblogCategories,IT,7` &format=`rss`!]`
Content Type	**text/xml**
Parent	**58** (The ID of your document—Getting to know ditto)

Now preview the pages and you will see something like the following:

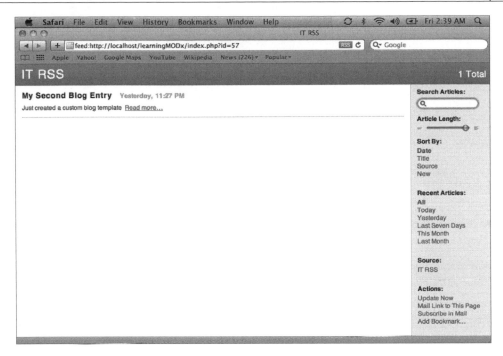

As you can see, each resource only lists the aggregation of blogs for a single category. Also notice that these resources use a different icon in the resource tree. This indicates that the document is an XML document:

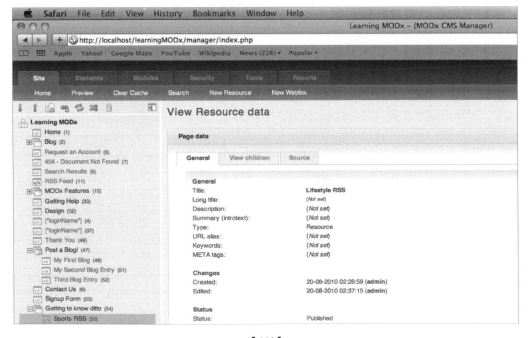

The snippet calls in the previous resources use parameters that we have already learned, except for the filter parameter which is explained in the following section.

Filtering

Ditto allows you to filter the resources being aggregated, based on filtering rules that you define. These rules are passed as a value in the parameter &filter. The format of the filter rule is

```
Field,criterion,mode
```

where:

- Field is any field from the resource, such as the ID or title; it can also be a template variable. If the field is a template variable, the field name must be prefixed with tv.
- criterion is any value with which you want to compare the field's value.
- mode is a number that defines what kind of comparison is to be performed.

The following is a list of all the possible comparisons:

Filter	Mode
is not equal to the criterion (!=)	1
is equal to the criterion (==)	2
is less than the criterion (<)	3
is greater than the criterion (>)	4
is less than or equal to the criterion (<=)	5
is greater than or equal to the criterion (>=)	6
does not contain the text of the criterion	7
does contain the text of the criterion	8

For example, if you want a resource with ID 2, you would write:

```
id,2,2
```

Each such rule is called a clause. id,2,2 forms a clause.

Multiple clauses

You can also have multiple filtering clauses by separating each clause with a | symbol. The | behaves like the or operator. If any one of the conditions is true, then the resource is retrieved.

For example, you may want all of the resources with an ID that is less than 4 and greater than 100.

The clause for all of the resources less than ID 4 would be:

```
id,4,3
```

From the previous table, mode 3 stands for "is less than the criterion". The clause means that you should use `id` as the criterion, and filter the resources that have the value for the criterion (`id`) as less than 4.

The clause for all of the resources greater than ID 100 would be:

```
id,100,4
```

From the preceding table, mode 4 stands for "is greater than the criterion". So, the rule to get the resources for both of the previous conditions would be:

```
id,4,3 | id,100,4
```

The whole expression to Ditto would be:

```
[!ditto? &someparametere... &filter=`id,4,3 | id,100,4`!]
```

Extenders

Ditto also allows developers to extend the functionality of Ditto by using new snippets. Such snippets are called **extenders**. There are a few Ditto extender snippets that were included in the installation of MODx. When you want to use an extender, you must tell Ditto which snippet to use by passing the name of the extender as an argument to the `&extenders` parameter.

Summary

In this chapter, you have learned about one very useful snippet, called Ditto. You have seen how to create aggregation and feeds, and how to create feeds for separate categories. You have also learned about tagging and how to tag resources and use them in MODx.

7
Creating Lists

MODx allows menus to be dynamically created, based on the content available, as resources. Menus are basically lists of resources, and submenus are lists of lists (lists within a menu list). In MODx, the simplest way to create lists of all the resources is by using the [[wayfinder]] snippet. In this chapter, we will learn how MODx allows us to create these lists dynamically, and also learn how to present them as menus.

Menu details in document properties

Every resource that can be shown in a menu must have the **Shown in Menu** option enabled in the resource's setting page. The **Resource setting** page also has two other options related to menus:

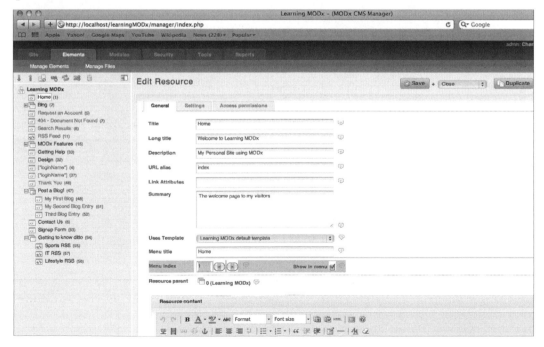

- **Menu title** — what to show in the menu. The resource title is used, if this value is left blank.

- **Menu index** — when a list of the resources that are to be listed in the menu is created, the menu index can be used to sort the resources in the required order. Menu index is a number, and when creating lists we can specify how we want to use the index.

Authentication and authorization

When creating the list of resources, **WayFinder** lists only those resources that are accessible by the user depending on the access permissions set for each resource, and the web user group to which the user belongs. For more information on access permissions, refer to *Chapter 5, Authentication and Authorization*.

Getting to know WayFinder

WayFinder is a snippet that outputs the structure of the resources as reflected in the resource tree. It creates the lists of all the resources that can be accessed by the current user, from those that been marked as **Shown in Menu** in the resource properties. Let's try out an exercise to discover WayFinder.

1. Create a new resource.
2. Set the name as **testing wayfinder**.
3. Choose the template as **(blank)**.
4. Place the following as the content:
   - ◦ `[[Wayfinder?startId=`0` ]]`
5. Save the document, and then preview it.

You will see a screen like the one shown in the following screenshot:

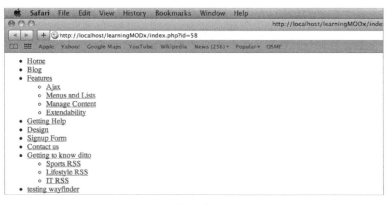

Notice that WayFinder has created a list of all of the resources, even the ones from the sample site. Each item is a link, so clicking on it leads you to the corresponding document. The generated HTML will look like the following example:

```
<ul><li><a href="http://localhost/learningMODx/" title="Home" >Home</
a></li>
<li><a href="/learningMODx/index.php?id=2" title="Blog" >Blog</a></li>
<li><a href="/learningMODx/index.php?id=15" title="MODx Features"
>Features</a><ul><li><a href="/learningMODx/index.php?id=16"
title="Ajax" >Ajax</a></li>
<li><a href="/learningMODx/index.php?id=22" title="Menus and Lists"
>Menus and Lists</a></li>
<li><a href="/learningMODx/index.php?id=14" title="Content Management"
>Manage Content</a></li>
<li class="last"><a href="/learningMODx/index.php?id=24"
title="Extendable by design" >Extendability</a></li>
</ul></li>
<li><a href="/learningMODx/index.php?id=33" title="Getting Help"
>Getting Help</a></li>
<li><a href="/learningMODx/index.php?id=32" title="Design" >Design</
a></li>
<li><a href="/learningMODx/index.php?id=53" title="Signup Form"
>Signup Form</a></li>
<li><a href="/learningMODx/index.php?id=6" title="Contact Us" >Contact
us</a></li>
<li><a href="/learningMODx/index.php?id=54" title="Getting to know
ditto" >Getting to know ditto</a><ul><li><a href="/learningMODx/index.
php?id=55" title="Sports RSS" >Sports RSS</a></li>
<li><a href="/learningMODx/index.php?id=56" title="Lifestyle RSS"
>Lifestyle RSS</a></li>
<li class="last"><a href="/learningMODx/index.php?id=57" title="IT
RSS" >IT RSS</a></li>
</ul></li>
<li class="last active"><a href="/learningMODx/index.php?id=58"
title="testing wayfinder" >testing wayfinder</a></li>
</ul>
```

As seen in the preceding output, the generated list is just a set of `<ul>` and `<li>` tags. Let's go step-by-step, in understanding how the preceding output can be customized and themed, starting with menus of one level.

Theming

To be able to theme the list generated by WayFinder to appear as menus, we need to understand how WayFinder works in more detail. In this section, we will show you step-by-step how to create a simple menu without any sub-items, and then proceed to creating menus with sub-items.

Creating a simple menu

Since, for now, we only want a menu without any submenu items, we have to show resources only from the top level of the resource tree. By default, WayFinder will reflect the complete structure of the resource tree, including the resources within containers, as seen in the preceding screenshot. WayFinder lets you choose the depth of the list via the &level parameter. The parameter &level takes a value indicating the number of levels that WayFinder should include in the menu. For our example, because we only want a simple menu with no submenu items, &level is set to 1.

Now, let us change the testing wayfinder resource, which we just created, to the following code:

```
[[Wayfinder?startId=`0` &level=`1` ]]
```

Preview the resource now, and you will see that the source code of the generated page in place of Wayfinder is:

```
<ul><li><a href="http://localhost/learningMODx/" title="Home" >Home</a></li>
<li><a href="/learningMODx/index.php?id=2" title="Blog" >Blog</a></li>
<li><a href="/learningMODx/index.php?id=15" title="MODx Features" >Features</a></li>
<li><a href="/learningMODx/index.php?id=33" title="Getting Help" >Getting Help</a></li>
<li><a href="/learningMODx/index.php?id=32" title="Design" >Design</a></li>
<li><a href="/learningMODx/index.php?id=53" title="Signup Form" >Signup Form</a></li>
<li><a href="/learningMODx/index.php?id=6" title="Contact Us" >Contact us</a></li>
<li><a href="/learningMODx/index.php?id=54" title="Getting to know ditto" >Getting to know ditto</a></li>
<li class="last active"><a href="/learningMODx/index.php?id=58" title="testing wayfinder" >testing wayfinder</a></li>
</ul>
```

Now, if we can just give <ul> and <li> respective classes, we can style them to appear as a menu. We can do this by passing the class names to the parameter &rowClass.

Change the contents of the preceding testing wayfinder to:

```
<div id="menu">
[!Wayfinder?startId=`0` &level=`1` &rowClass=`menu`!]
</div>
```

Now, open `style.css` from the `root` folder, and change the CSS to the following code. What we are doing is styling the preceding generated list to appear like a menu, by using CSS:

```css
* { padding:2; margin:0; border:1; }
body { margin:0 20px; background:#8CEC81; }
#banner { background: #2BB81B; border-top:5px solid #8CEC81; border-
                                   bottom:5px solid #8CEC81; }
#banner h1 { padding:10px; }
#wrapper { background: #8CEC81; }
#container { width: 100%; background: #2BB81B; float: left; }
#content { background: #ffffff; height:600px; padding:0 10px 10px
                                   10px; clear:both; }
#footer { background: #2BB81B; border-top:5px solid #8CEC81; border-
                                   bottom:5px solid #8CEC81; }
.clearing { clear:both; height:0; }
#content #col-1 {float:left;width:500px; margin:0px;padding:0px;}
#content #col-2 {float:right; width:300px; margin:0px; padding:30px 0
          10px 25px; border-left:3px solid #99cc66; height:500px;}
#content #col-2 div {padding-bottom:20px;}

#menu {
background:#ffffff;
float: left;
}

#menu ul {
list-style: none;
margin: 0;
padding: 0;
width: 48em;
float: left;
}

#menu ul li {
display: inline;
}
#menu a, #menu h2 {
font: bold 11px/16px arial, helvetica, sans-serif;
display: inline;
border-width: 1px;
border-style: solid;
border-color: #ccc #888 #555 #bbb;
margin: 0;
padding: 2px 3px;
}
#menu h2 {
color: #fff;
background: #000;
```

```
text-transform: uppercase;
}
#menu a {
color: #000;
background: #2BB81B;
text-decoration: none;
}
#menu a:hover {
color: #2BB81B;
background: #fff;
}
```

Also remember to change the template of the resource to the learning MODx default template.

Now preview the page, and you will see something like the one shown in the following screenshot:

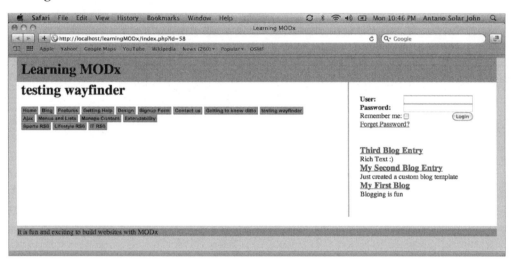

The HTML code returned will be similar to the following:

```
<ul><li class="menu"><a href="http://localhost/learningMODx/"
title="Home" >Home</a></li>
<li class="menu"><a href="/learningMODx/index.php?id=2" title="Blog"
>Blog</a></li>
<li class="menu"><a href="/learningMODx/index.php?id=15" title="MODx
Features" >Features</a></li>
<li class="menu"><a href="/learningMODx/index.php?id=33"
title="Getting Help" >Getting Help</a></li>
<li class="menu"><a href="/learningMODx/index.php?id=32"
title="Design" >Design</a></li>
<li class="menu"><a href="/learningMODx/index.php?id=53" title="Signup
Form" >Signup Form</a></li>
```

```
<li class="menu"><a href="/learningMODx/index.php?id=6" title="Contact
Us" >Contact us</a></li>
<li class="menu"><a href="/learningMODx/index.php?id=54"
title="Getting to know ditto" >Getting to know ditto</a></li>
<li class="menu last active"><a href="/learningMODx/index.php?id=58"
title="testing wayfinder" >testing wayfinder</a></li>
</ul>
```

Notice that for each menu item, the class menu has been applied. Although we have not applied any custom style to the menu class, we have shown you that when you are building more fine-grained menu systems, you have the ability to have every item associated with a class.

Nested menus

When we have more than one level of the menu structure, we will want different styling for the top menu and the menu items. This effectively means that we need to have different classes for different levels. Also, some menu systems have different styling for the first and the last elements. Such flexibility in styling is also possible with the WayFinder snippet. Let us consider a two-level structure with the class names that we might want illustrated, shown at the side. For this example, the list will be:

```
<ul>
  <li> Menu1 Name </li>                outer first
    <ul>
      <li> Menu item 1</li>            inner first
      <li>Menu item 2</li>            inner
      <li>Menu item 3</li>            inner
      <li>Menu item 4</li>            inner last
    </ul>
  <li> Menu2 Name</li>                outer
    <ul>
      <li> Menu item 1</li>            inner first
      <li>Menu item 2</li>            inner
      <li>Menu item 3</li>            inner
      <li>Menu item 4</li>            inner last
    </ul>
  <li> Menu3 Name</li>                outer last
    <ul>
      <li> Menu item 1</li>            inner first
      <li>Menu item 2</li>            inner
      <li>Menu item 3</li>            inner
      <li>Menu item 4</li>            inner last
    </ul>
</ul>
```

The following are the list of parameters that we will need to use to be able to have the respective class names in the generated list:

Parameter	Definition
&firstClass	CSS class denoting the first item at a given menu level
&lastClass	CSS class denoting the last item at a given menu level
&hereClass	CSS class denoting the "you are here" state, all the way up the chain
&selfClass	CSS class denoting the "you are here" state, for only the current doc
&parentClass	CSS class denoting that the menu item is a folder (has children)
&rowClass	CSS class denoting each output row
&levelClass	CSS class denoting each output row's level; the level number will be added to the specified class (that is, level1, level2, level3, and so on)
&outerClass	CSS class for the outer template
&innerClass	CSS class for the inner template
&webLinkClass	CSS class for weblinks

Now change the content in the testing wayfinder document to:

```
<div id="menu">
[!Wayfinder?startId=`0` &level=`2` &outerClass=`outer`
&innerClass='inner' &lastClass=`last` &firstClass=`first`
&hereClass=`active`!]
</div>
```

This code will result in an output similar to the following code. Notice that the class names are similar to the structure that we wanted, as outlined earlier.

```
div id="menu">
<ul class="outer"><li class="first"><a href="http://localhost/
learningMODx/" title="Home" >Home</a></li>
<li><a href="/learningMODx/index.php?id=2" title="Blog" >Blog</a></li>
<li><a href="/learningMODx/index.php?id=15" title="MODx Features"
>Features</a><ul class="'inner'"><li class="first"><a href="/
learningMODx/index.php?id=16" title="Ajax" >Ajax</a></li>
<li><a href="/learningMODx/index.php?id=22" title="Menus and Lists"
>Menus and Lists</a></li>
<li><a href="/learningMODx/index.php?id=14" title="Content Management"
>Manage Content</a></li>
<li class="last"><a href="/learningMODx/index.php?id=24"
title="Extendable by design" >Extendability</a></li>
</ul></li>
<li><a href="/learningMODx/index.php?id=33" title="Getting Help"
>Getting Help</a></li>
<li><a href="/learningMODx/index.php?id=32" title="Design" >Design</
a></li>
```

```
<li><a href="/learningMODx/index.php?id=53" title="Signup Form"
>Signup Form</a></li>
<li><a href="/learningMODx/index.php?id=6" title="Contact Us" >Contact
us</a></li>
<li><a href="/learningMODx/index.php?id=54" title="Getting to
know ditto" >Getting to know ditto</a><ul class="'inner'"><li
class="first"><a href="/learningMODx/index.php?id=55" title="Sports
RSS" >Sports RSS</a></li>
<li><a href="/learningMODx/index.php?id=56" title="Lifestyle RSS"
>Lifestyle RSS</a></li>
<li class="last"><a href="/learningMODx/index.php?id=57" title="IT
RSS" >IT RSS</a></li>
</ul></li>
<li class="last active"><a href="/learningMODx/index.php?id=58"
title="testing wayfinder" >testing wayfinder</a></li>
</ul>
</div>
```

Now preview the page, and it will look like the one shown in the following screenshot:

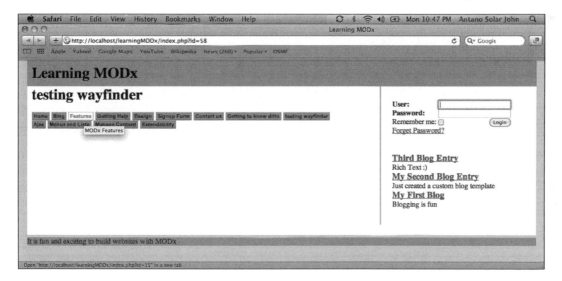

Notice that the inner items are also shown. We will change this behavior by adding some CSS styling to show this inner menu only on hover.

Now, edit `style.css` to be the following:

```
* { padding:2; margin:0; border:1; }
body { margin:0 20px; background:#8CEC81; }
#banner { background: #2BB81B; border-top:5px solid #8CEC81; border-
                                    bottom:5px solid #8CEC81; }
#banner h1 { padding:10px; }
```

```css
#wrapper { background: #8CEC81; }
#container { width: 100%; background: #2BB81B; float: left; }
#content { background: #ffffff; height:600px; padding:0 10px 10px
                                        10px; clear:both; }
#footer { background: #2BB81B; border-top:5px solid #8CEC81; border-
                                   bottom:5px solid #8CEC81; }
.clearing { clear:both; height:0; }
#content #col-1 {float:left;width:500px; margin:0px;padding:0px;}
#content #col-2 {float:right; width:300px; margin:0px; padding:30px 0
            10px 25px; border-left:3px solid #99cc66; height:500px;}
#content #col-2 div {padding-bottom:20px;}
#menu {
background:#ffffff;
float: left;
}
#menu ul {
list-style: none;
margin: 0;
padding: 0;
width: 48em;
float: left;
}
#menu ul li {
display: inline;
}
#menu a, #menu h2 {
font: bold 11px/16px arial, helvetica, sans-serif;
display: inline;
border-width: 1px;
border-style: solid;
border-color: #ccc #888 #555 #bbb;
margin: 0;
padding: 2px 3px;
}
#menu h2 {
color: #fff;
background: #000;
text-transform: uppercase;
}
#menu a {
color: #000;
background: #2BB81B;
text-decoration: none;
}
#menu a:hover {
color: #2BB81B;
background: #fff;
```

```
}
#menu li {position: relative;}
#menu ul ul {
position: relative;
z-index: 500;
}
#menu ul ul ul {
top: 0;
left: 100%;
}
div#menu ul ul,
div#menu ul li:hover ul ul,
div#menu ul ul li:hover ul ul
{display: none;}
div#menu ul li:hover ul,
div#menu ul ul li:hover ul,
div#menu ul ul ul li:hover ul
{display: block;}
```

Now preview the page and note that the submenu items are shown only on hover. This is also shown in the next screenshot.

Note again that the class name generated previously is only for information purposes. This is to let you know that you have a finer-grained menu system available to you if you need it. Had you replaced the call to Wayfinder with just [!Wayfinder?startId=`0` &level=`2`!], it would have still worked.

Now that we have the menus appearing in this page, let us make them appear in all the pages. Note that we created this page only for testing, and to find out how WayFinder works. We will need to use the code that we have come up with in this page in the default Learning MODx template.

Change the default Learning MODx template to the following:

```
<!DOCTYPE html PUBLIC "-//W3C//DTD XHTML 1.1//EN" "http://www.w3.org/
TR/xhtml11/DTD/xhtml11.dtd"> <html xmlns="http://www.w3.org/1999/
xhtml" xml:lang="en">
<head>
  <base href="[(site_url)]"></base>
  <title>Learning MODx</title>
  <meta http-equiv="Content-Type" content="text/html;
charset=iso-8859-1" />
  <link rel="stylesheet" type="text/css" href="assets/templates/
learningMODx/style.css" />
</head>
<body>
  <div id="banner">
```

```
   <h1>Learning MODx</h1>
 </div>
 <div id="wrapper">
  <div id="container">
   <div id="content">
    <div id="col-1">
    <div id="menu">
        [!Wayfinder?startId=`0` &level=`2` &outerClass=`outer`
&innerClass='inner' &lastClass=`last` &firstClass=`first`
&hereClass=`active`!]
     </div>

     <h1>[*pagetitle*]</h1>
     <br/>
     [*#content*]
    </div>
    <div id="col-2" >
     <div > [!WebLogin!] </div>
      <div>
       [!Ditto? &parents=`47` &tpl=`dittofrontpage`!]
      </div>

    </div>
   </div>
  </div>
  <div class="clearing"> </div>
 </div> <!-- end of wrapper div -->
 <div id="footer">It is fun and exciting to build websites with
                                        MODx</div></body>
</html>
```

Save the template, and then preview the **Home** page. It will look like the example shown in the following screenshot:

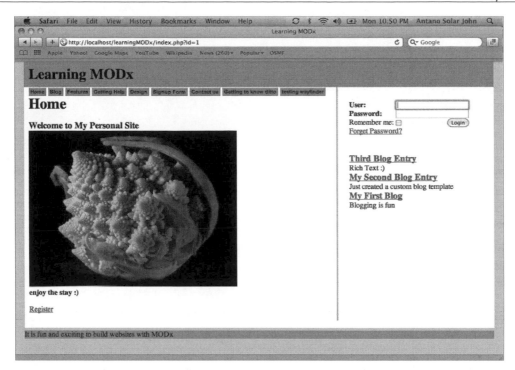

Now that you have learned how to theme lists that are two levels deep, you may be wondering how to theme lists that are more than two-levels deep. You can theme such lists by using the `levelClass` parameter. For example, if you set `&levelClass` = `level`, then the level items will have the classes `level1`, `level2`, `level3`.

```
[!Wayfinder?startId=`0` &level=`5` &outerClass=`outer`
&innerClass='inner' &lastClass=`last` &firstClass=`first`
&hereClass=`active` &level2=`xxx` &level3=`yyy`!]
```

Changing the name in the menu

Let us change the name of the menu title for the page called 'Getting to know ditto', which lists all of the blog entries, that we had created in the previous chapter when we learned to use template variables for tagging in RSS format. To do that, perform the following steps:

1. Click on the resource **Getting to know ditto** and edit it.

2. Change the menu title to **Feeds**.

3. Save the document.

4. Repeat the above steps for the document **SignUp Form** and change the menu name to **Register**.

Notice that the menus have changed, as shown in the following screenshot:

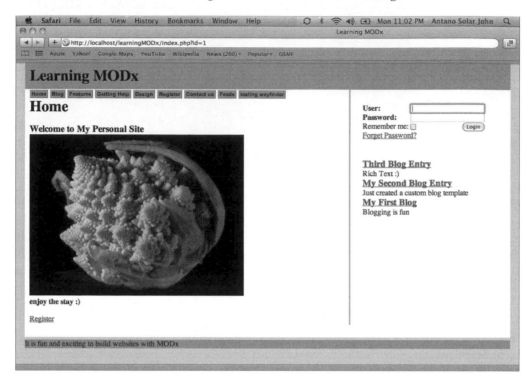

Doc Manager

Doc Manager is a module that allows you to change the template, template variables, and other resource properties of one or more resources. Using the Doc Manager makes it easier to make changes to multiple resources simultaneously. Doc Manager can be accessed from the **Doc Manager** menu item in the **Modules** menu. The following is a screenshot of the Doc Manager:

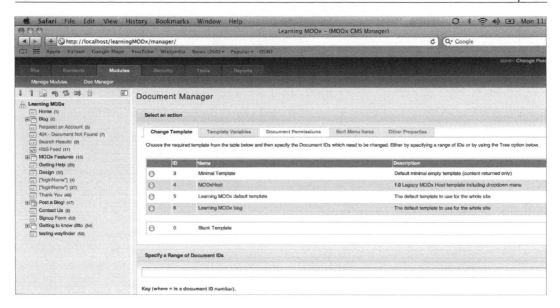

As you can see, it has five tabs:

Tab Name	Functionality
Change Template	Change the template of one or more resources
Template Variables	Change the values in the template variables for one or more resources
Document Permissions	Add or remove one or more resource to or from a resource group
Sort Menu Items	Provide a drag-and-drop menu ordering functionality for the child resources of a selected parent
Other Properties	Set resource dates, authors, and other Yes/No options, such as cacheable, published, and so on, for one or more documents

Following is a screenshot of **Sort Menu Items** after selecting the **Parent** as **Learning MODx**(0) - the root folder. The parent for sort menu items was selected done by clicking on it and then clicking on **Go**.

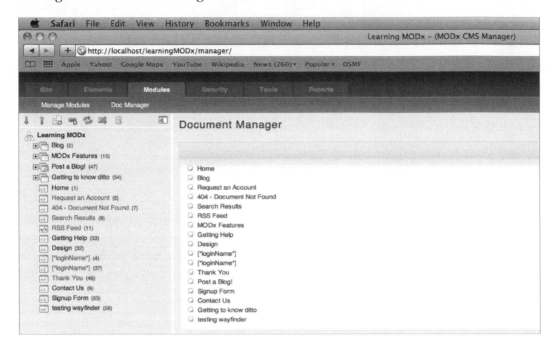

Note that this module still calls resources as documents, as they were called in earlier versions of MODx. So you can safely substitute the word document with resource when you come across it here in this module.

With the exception of **Sort Menu Items**, all actions have a field at the bottom called **Specify a Range of Document IDs**.

The resources on which the changes have to be made are selected by entering the appropriate value in this field. You can specify a single resource, or a range of resources, with the operator. You can refer to a resource and all of its immediate children by entering the resource ID followed by an *. You can specify a resource and all its children by entering the resource ID followed by **. You can have a list of all of these syntaxes, as long as they are separated by commas; for example: 10,20-30,5*,8**. This will make the selected changes in:

- Resource 10
- Resources 20 to resource 30
- Resource 5 and all of its immediate children
- Resource 8 and all of its children

Removing pages from the menu

You might notice that menu items are generated even for pages from the MODx sample site. Because our purpose for having these pages is only to look at them and learn, we do not want them to be appearing in our menus. Also, there are a few pages that we have created to test the functionality; and we will want to hide these, too. You can hide resources one by one by selecting the resource, clicking on **Edit**, deselecting the **Shown in Menu** checkbox, and then saving the resource. Alternatively, you can use the Doc Manager to change the properties for a set of documents.

To change the **Shown in Menu** setting using the Doc Manager, carry out the following steps:

1. Click on the **Modules** menu, and then select the **Doc Manager** menu item.
2. Click on the **Other Properties** tab.
3. Change the **Available Settings** to **Show/Hide in Menu**.
4. Select the **Hide in Menu** checkbox.
5. In the **Specify a Range of Document IDs** field, list the IDs for all of the documents that you want to hide separated by commas. It can be something like 2*,15*,33,39*,32,6,58. Notice that * stands for the document with the given ID and its immediate children.

Note that the preceding ID list could be different for you depending on the order in which you created the documents.

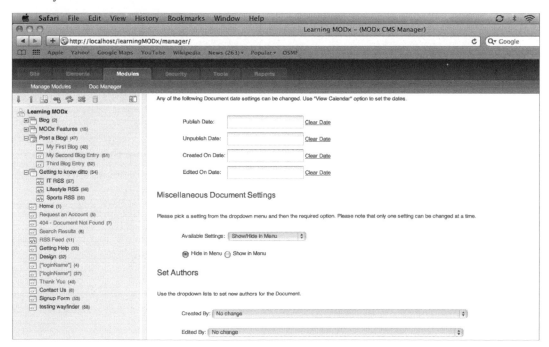

Now click on **Preview** and the page will look like the example shown in the following screenshot:

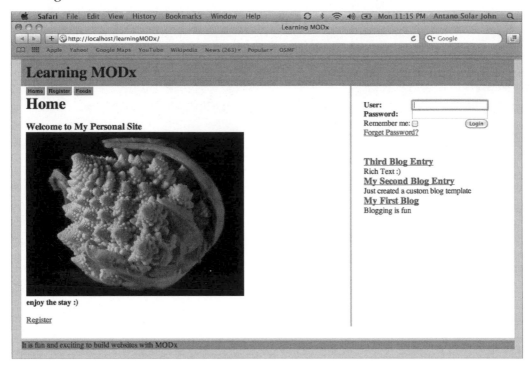

More theming using chunks

Now that we have learned how to give custom class names for generated `<ul>` `<li>` unordered lists, we are able to theme them by having the corresponding styles for the classes. What if we wanted to have a list that is not a `<ul>` `<li>` type? Alternatively, what if we wanted to have more control over how the list is generated? WayFinder also allows the user to customize the structure of the generated lists, by using chunks. Similar to the use of custom classes, WayFinder has separate parameters that specify which chunk to use for which level, and so on. As with any chunk, the dynamic content comes from the available placeholders that are set by the snippet (in this case it is WayFinder). In this section, we will look at breadcrumbs and discuss the parameters that are used for creating the breadcrumb trail.

Breadcrumb navigation

Breadcrumbs are those small links that you generally see at the top of a page that help you to understand which part of the site you are in and how you got there.

For example, if you are accessing a blog entry inside a `blog` folder, then the breadcrumb would be:

```
home>>blog>>blogname
```

In the preceding example, `home` and `blog` are links to take you to the roots of the current document.

Following is the code and an explanation of how breadcrumbs can be created in MODx using WayFinder.

```
<a href="/" title="Home">Home</a> &raquo; [!Wayfinder? &startId=`0`
&outerTpl=`BreadCrumbOuter` &rowTpl=`BreadCrumbRow` &activeParentRowTp
l=`BreadCrumbActiveParentRow` &hereTpl=`BreadCrumbHere`!]
```

`&raquo` gets converted to `>>`. The previous call to `Wayfinder` uses different chunks for different levels in order to process and create the list. It will be easier to understand the wrapper placeholders if you remember the following concepts:

- The call to `WayFinder` generates resource lists based on the given parameters
- For each resource in the resource list, the placeholders in the appropriate chunk are replaced by the values from the resource
- The chunks being used are determined by the value of the corresponding snippet parameter
- The innermost document list is generated first, and then it is followed by the outermost document list

Parameter	Given Chunk Name	For what items the chunk will be called	Code for the chunk	Explanation of the code
`&outertpl`	Bread CrumbOuter	When processing the outmost container. (What it should be instead of `<ul>` `</ul>` for the outermost level.)	`[+wf.wrapper+]`	The template variable `[+wf.wrapper+]` specifies where the innermost content will be inserted.
`&rowTpl`	Bread Crumbrow	When processing each resource in the resource list. (What it should be instead of `<li> </li>` for every level.)		We leave it empty, as for the breadcrumb, we want only the current item and the parent item of the current item to be shown.

Parameter	Given Chunk Name	For what items the chunk will be called	Code for the chunk	Explanation of the code
`Active ParentRowTpl`	`BreadCrumb Active ParentRow`	When processing the parent resource of the current resource.	`<a href="[+wf. link+]" title="[+wf. title+]">[+wf. linktext+]</a> &raquo; [+wf. wrapper+]`	We display a link for the parent resource by using the placeholders for `link`, `title`, and `linktext`. Then we specify where the inner contents should be inserted. (If it is a parent resource, it definitely has at least the current resource as the inner level resource.)
`&hereTpl`	`Bread CrumbHere`	When processing the current resource.	`[+wf.linktext+]`	We show the current resource's menu title here, as we do not want a link to the resource when we are already on that page.

Multiple calls

It is possible to have *multiple calls* to WayFinder within the same document or template. This might be necessary when you want to have multiple menu systems in the same page. For instance, you might want to have a primary menu at the top and additional menus on the left or right. You can have one call to WayFinder for the menus, one for the breadcrumb trail, and so on. To do this, you will only have to place the corresponding WayFinder snippet calls at the appropriate positions in the template being used.

Example structure:

HTML

```
    <!-- WayFinder snippet call for breadcrumbs -->
<a href="/" title="Home">Home</a> &raquo; [!Wayfinder? &startId=`0`
&outerTpl=`BreadCrumbOuter` &rowTpl=`BreadCrumbRow` &activeParentRowTp
l=`BreadCrumbActiveParentRow` &hereTpl=`BreadCrumbHere
```

HTML

```
    <!-- WayFinder snippet  call for menu ->
[!Wayfinder?startId=`0` &level=`2` &outerClass=`outer`
&innerClass='inner' &lastClass=`last` &firstClass=`first`
&hereClass=`active`!]
```

Summary

We have learned how to use the snippet `[[WayFinder]]` to create lists of documents. We also saw how the snippet parameters for WayFinder make the list creation flexible. All WayFinder parameters help in doing one of the following three actions:

- **Filtering**— to what list?
- **Styling**—which style classes do I use for the default or custom lists?
- **Structuring**—which chunk defines my list structure?

We have seen examples for filtering, styling, and structuring. In the process, we have also added a menu system for our site. We have also learned how to use the Doc Manager module to change the properties of a group of documents quickly, without having to do them one by one.

8
Snippets

We have been using snippets throughout this book without much detail on what they really are. In this chapter, you will learn more about snippets. We will explore the snippets that come with MODx and those that are available for downloading. You will learn how to install a snippet, use a snippet, and navigate its custom functionalities. As an example, we will be looking at one snippet called Jot and use it to allow comments on posts.

Working of snippets

Snippets are units of code that can be called from a resource or a template.

A snippet can do one or more of the following three things:

- Return text or HTML
- Populate template variables
- Process a chunk and return its value

Almost anything that can be done in PHP can be done using a snippet. However, how you control the output and the flexibility of the snippet depends on how you use the snippet to do one of the preceding activities or a combination of them.

A snippet can be called by using one of the following notations:

- [[snippetname]] —cached call
- [!snippetname!] —non-cached call

In a cached call, a snippet is processed once, and whatever it generates is cached and used till the cache is cleared. However, if the page from which the snippet is executed is not cached, the snippet will be processed anyway for every request. Caching may be useful for optimization in situations where the expected output from the snippet does not change frequently.

In a non-cached call, a snippet is processed each time the page loads. Hence, there is no speed optimization by cache for the snippet. This may be necessary for snippets interacting with forms where the processed output is going to be dynamic every time. Also, a page can be cached and only the snippet can be non-cached. This way the optimization for the whole page is still retained. All of this was already explained in *Chapter 5, Authentication and Authorization*.

Finding snippets

Whenever you want to add new functionality to a site, the first step is to find an appropriate snippet that can provide the site with such functionality. There are a few snippets that come packaged with MODx, in which case you don't have to install them. We will see one example of such a snippet in this section. In a later section of this chapter, you will learn how to install new snippets.

Now, let us consider how to add comments to blog entries. Searching in Google for *MODx comments* brings the page `http://wiki.MODxcms.com/index.php/Jot` as one of the first links. This page shows us that `Jot` is a snippet that can be used for adding comments to blogs. Note that in this case I have listed the name of the snippet. However, there are literally hundreds of snippets, and the list of contributed snippets is growing rapidly. So it is really necessary that you learn how to search for the best snippet that will get you what you want. You might also want to search for snippets in the MODx repository and on the MODx forums.

Learning about snippets

Now we have identified that we want to use the `Jot` snippet. What next?

- Try out the snippet with the minimal configuration
- Check the list of available parameters
- Use placeholders if it involves HTML that can be processed from a chunk

An explanation for each of the preceding points follows. Note that this section is not specifically about `Jot`, but rather about learning how to use a new snippet.

Jot with the minimal configuration

Whenever you want to learn how to use a snippet, it is a good idea to try it out with the minimal configuration needed. This way, you can be sure that your understanding of what the snippet does is correct. Reading through the page that we have just found (in the wiki documentation), it doesn't seem like there are any required parameters, and all parameters seem optional. So let us just go and place the Jot call below the posts in the blog template.

Edit the Learning MODx blog template and add the highlighted call to Jot, so that the template code looks like the following:

```
<!DOCTYPE html PUBLIC "-//W3C//DTD XHTML 1.1//EN"  "http://www.w3.org/
TR/xhtml11/DTD/xhtml11.dtd">
<html xmlns="http://www.w3.org/1999/xhtml" xml:lang="en">
<head>
<title>Learning Modx</title>
<meta http-equiv="Content-Type" content="text/html;
charset=iso-8859-1" />
<link rel="stylesheet" type="text/css" href="assets/templates/
learningMODx/style.css" />
</head>
<body>
<div id="banner">
<h1>Learning MODx</h1>
</div>
<div id="wrapper">
<div id="container">
  <div id="content">
    [*pagetitle*]
    <br/>
    [*#content*]
    <br/>
    [!Jot!]
  </div>
</div>
  <div class="clearing"></div>
</div> <!-- end of wrapper div -->
<div id="footer">It is fun and exciting to build websites with
                                    MODx</div></body>
</html>
```

Now preview any of the posted blogs and it will look like the example shown in the following screenshot:

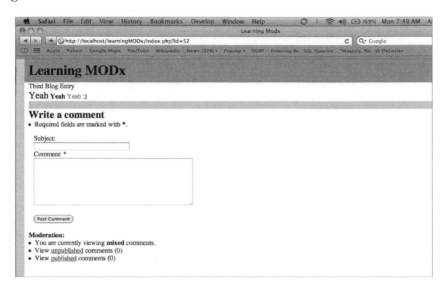

To change the default form, we have to find the parameter for the snippet that we can use to specify the chunk to use. Then we need to learn which placeholders can be used in the chunk. Let's test if Jot is actually working by posting a comment. Following is a screenshot of how it looks after posting a comment.

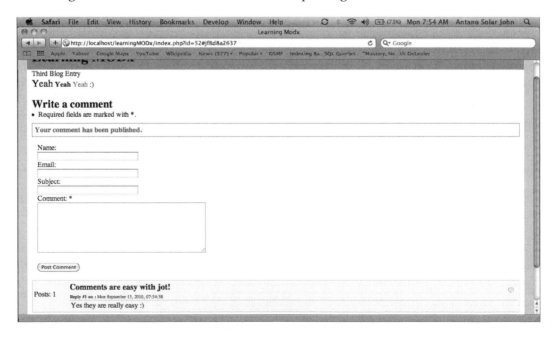

Note that some snippets vary their functionality based on whether you are logged in as a manager or not. Log out from the Manager interface, refresh the page, and it will appear like the example shown in the following screenshot:

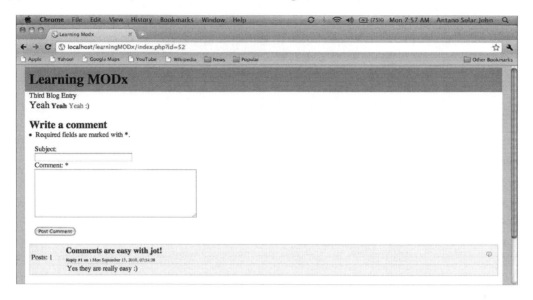

Notice that the moderation links are missing in this screen.

Snippet parameters

Snippet parameters, as you have already learned, are what allow you to control the functionality of a snippet. A parameter takes one or more value after the = sign. The parameter itself is preceded by an &.

Now, have a look at the available `Jot` parameters , as listed on the web page given earlier. We want to configure the behavior of `Jot` in two ways, and hence we need to identify the appropriate parameters to configure it.

- Restrict comments to authenticated users — `&canpost`
- Theme the comment form — `&tplForm`

The value that has to be passed to `&tplForm` is the name of the HTML chunk to be used for the form. `&canpost` takes a comma-separated list of the names of the groups that are allowed to post comments. Now let us change the highlighted call to `Jot`, in the preceding code of the `Learning MODx` blog template, to the following:

```
[!Jot? &canpost=`Registered Users`!]
```

Now log out of the Web interface, log out of the Manager interface, and preview the blog page. It will appear like the example shown in the following screenshot:

You won't see the comment form. This is because of the preceding call where we specified that only allow registered users should see the comment form, by assigning `&canpost=`Registered Users` in the Jot snippet call.

Now log in through the Web interface as samira, the user that you created in a *Chapter 5, Authentication and Authorization,* and the page looks like the example shown in the following screenshot:

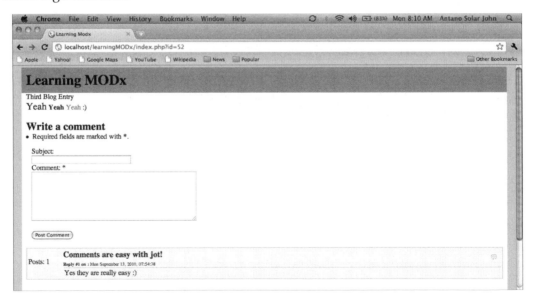

As you can see, the comments form is now available. If you still do not see the comment form, click on the user **samira** from the admin manager and make sure the user is assigned to the Registered Users group.

Now that we have achieved the first of our two objectives (to restrict comments to registered users), let's get started with the second objective (theming the comment form). First, we need to specify which chunk to use as the custom form. For this, modify the preceding call to `Jot` to the following.

```
[!Jot? &tplForm=`comments` &canpost=`Registered Users`!]
```

Preview any comment page and it should look like the example shown in the following screenshot:

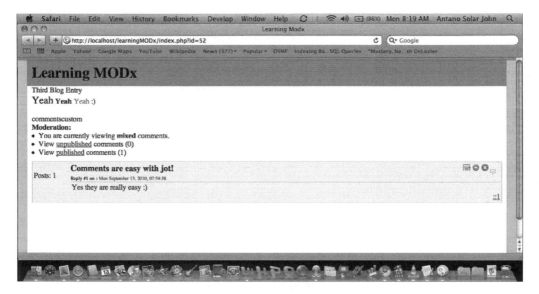

Notice that instead of the comments custom form, we see the static text comments. This is because `Jot` was unable to find the chunk named `comments`. Now, just for demonstration purposes, let us create a chunk with the following details:

Field Name	Value
Name	commentscustom
Content	Testing the comment form
Category	Learning MODx

If you preview the page now, it will look like the example shown in the following screenshot:

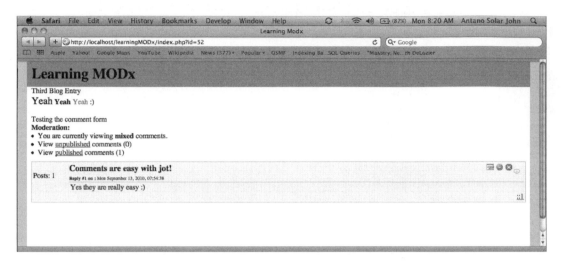

As you can see, the static text from the chunk comments, "Testing the comment form" has been replaced. Now, instead of this static text, what we require is a form that Jot can understand. In the case of Jot, there is no documentation, as of the time of writing, on how to write a form chunk for Jot. When you come across situations like this, you can understand what a snippet expects in a custom form by opening its own default templates. The wiki documentation states that the default templates are in the jot/ template directory. The next section of this chapter has more details on this. For now, just understand that we are opening a file named chunk.form.inc.html from the assests/snippets/jot/templates/, and this file has the following code:

```
<a name="jf[+jot.link.id+]"></a>
<h2>[+form.edit:is=`1`:then=`Edit comment`:else=`Write a comment`+]</
h2>
<div class="jot-list">
<ul>
  <li>Required fields are marked with <b>*</b>.</li>
</ul>
</div>
[+form.error:isnt=`0`:then=`
<div class="jot-err">
[+form.error:select=`
&-3=You are trying to re-submit the same post. You have probably
clicked the submit button more than once.
&-2=Your comment has been rejected.
&-1=Your comment has been saved, it will first be reviewed before it
is published.
```

```
&1=You are trying to re-submit the same post. You have probably
clicked the submit button more than once.
&2=The security code you entered was incorrect.
&3=You can only post once each [+jot.postdelay+] seconds.
&4=Your comment has been rejected.
&5=[+form.errormsg:ifempty=`You didn't enter all the required
fields`+]
+]
</div>
:strip+]
[+form.confirm:isnt=`0`:then=`
<div class="jot-cfm">
[+form.confirm:select=`
&1=Your comment has been published.
&2=Your comment has been saved, it will first be reviewed before it is
published.
&3=Comment saved.
`+]
</div>
`:strip+]
<form method="post" action="[+form.action:esc+]#jf[+jot.link.id+]"
class="jot-form">
  <fieldset>
  <input name="JotForm" type="hidden" value="[+jot.id+]" />
  <input name="JotNow" type="hidden" value="[+jot.seed+]" />
  <input name="parent" type="hidden" value="[+form.field.parent+]" />

  [+form.moderation:is=`1`:then=`
    <div class="jot-row">
      <b>Created on:</b> [+form.field.createdon:date=`%a %B %d, %Y at
%H:%M`+]<br />
      <b>Created by:</b> [+form.field.createdby:userinfo=`username`:if
empty=`[+jot.guestname+]`+]<br />
      <b>IP address:</b> [+form.field.secip+]<br />
      <b>Published:</b> [+form.field.published:select=`0=No&1=Yes`+]<
br />
      [+form.field.publishedon:gt=`0`:then=`
        <b>Published on:</b> [+form.field.publishedon:date=`%a %B %d,
%Y at %H:%M`+]<br />
        <b>Published by:</b> [+form.field.publishedby:userinfo=`userna
me`:ifempty=` - `+]<br />
        `+]
      [+form.field.editedon:gt=`0`:then=`
        <b>Edited on:</b> [+form.field.editedon:date=`%a %B %d, %Y at
%H:%M`+]<br />
```

```
        <b>Edited by:</b> [+form.field.editedby:userinfo=`username`:if
empty=` -`+]<br />
        `+]
    </div>
  `:strip+]

  [+form.guest:is=`1`:then=`
    <label for="name[+jot.id+]">Name:<br />
    <input tabindex="[+jot.seed:math=`?+1`+]" name="name" type="text"
size="40" value="[+form.field.custom.name:esc+]" id="name[+jot.id+]"
/>
    </label>
    <label for="email[+jot.id+]">Email:<br />
    <input tabindex="[+jot.seed:math=`?+2`+]" name="email" type="text"
size="40" value="[+form.field.custom.email:esc+]" id="email[+jot.
id+]"/>
    </label>
  `:strip+]

  <label for="title[+jot.id+]">Subject:<br />
  <input tabindex="[+jot.seed:math=`?+3`+]" name="title" type="text"
size="40" value="[+form.field.title:esc+]" id="title[+jot.id+]"/>
  </label>
  <label for="content[+jot.id+]">Comment: *<br />
  <textarea tabindex="[+jot.seed:math=`?+4`+]" name="content"
cols="50" rows="8" id="content[+jot.id+]">[+form.field.content:esc+]</
textarea>
  </label><br />

  [+jot.captcha:is=`1`:then=`
    <div style="width:150px;margin-top: 5px;margin-bottom: 5px;"><a
href="[+jot.link.current:esc+]"><img src="[(base_url)]manager/
includes/veriword.php?rand=[+jot.seed+]" width="148" height="60"
alt="If you have trouble reading the code, click on the code itself
to generate a new random code." style="border: 1px solid #003399" /></
a></div>
    <label for="vericode[+jot.id+]">Help prevent spam - enter
security code above:<br /><input type="text" name="vericode"
style="width:150px;" size="20" id="vericode[+jot.id+]" /></
label> 
  `:strip+]

  <div style="float:right;width: 100px;"></div>
  <input tabindex="[+jot.seed:math=`?+5`+]" name="submit"
type="submit" value="[+form.edit:is=`1`:then=`Save Comment`:else=`Post
Comment`+]" />
  [+form.edit:is=`1`:then=`
    <input tabindex="[+jot.seed:math=`?+5`+]" name="submit"
type="submit" value="Cancel" onclick="history.go(-1);return false;" />
```

```
`+]
    </fieldset>
</form>
```

Let us test what we have learned by just copying this code without any change to the `comments` chunk, and then preview it. You will see the same form that you saw before, but using a custom chunk.

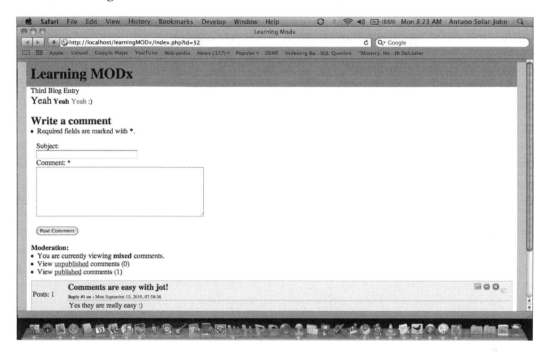

The preceding template uses PHx, which is explained in the next chapter. For now, let us just make a simple modification to the rendered form. Modify the chunk comments in line two from:

```
<h2>[+form.edit:is=`1`:then=`Edit comment`:else=`Write a
                                        comment`+]</h2>
```

to:

```
<b>[+form.edit:is=`1`:then=`Edit comment`:else=`Write a
                                        comment`+]</b>
```

Preview any comments page and it will look similar to the example shown in the following screenshot:

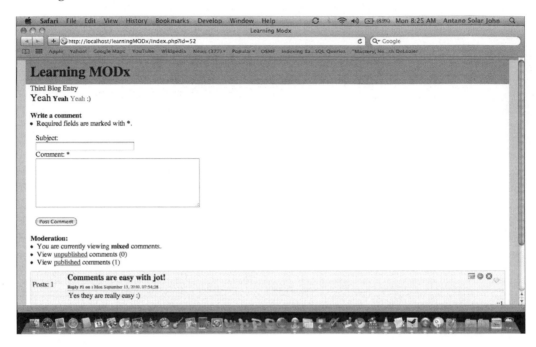

We have successfully changed the appearance of a specific element of the form from a heading to just bold text. Although we have changed only one line, using the same principles that you have just learned, you can change the appearance of the form to make it look any way you like.

Placeholders

Placeholders are similar to variables that can be placed within a chunk or a template. In the place of the placeholder, whatever value the snippet assigns to the placeholder will be inserted into the chunk or template during the processing of the snippet code. As we have already seen, most snippets provide placeholders that can be used in an HTML document, such as the `wayfinder` snippet, which we came across earlier in the previous chapter on lists.

Snippets like Jot provide many uses for placeholders. In the case of Jot, it has a comment form and the comments themselves. Maybe you want to change the order in which the details of comments are displayed by default. To do this, we can provide appropriate parameters to tell Jot to not output anything, but rather to set values for the placeholders that contain the details for the individual elements. Then we can place those placeholders in the templates in the order that we want. As an example, by default the comments are shown below the comment form. Let us go ahead and change this behavior to show the comments form after the comments. The first step is to let Jot know that we are not expecting one whole output that gets inserted in the place where Jot was called, but rather we want the separate elements to be placed in the placeholders. To do that, change the call to Jot in the Learning MODx blog template to contain &placeholders=`1` & output=`0`.

```
[!Jot? &placeholders=`1` &output=`0` &tplForm=`comments`
                   &canpost=`Registered Users`!]
```

Now if you preview any post, you will notice that the comments and the comment form have disappeared. This is as good as not having made a call to Jot at all. However, there is one difference, which is that now we have placeholders that contain the output, and we can place these placeholders anywhere in the template.

A few of the available Jot placeholders are:

- [+jot.html.navigation+] — places the navigation on the page
- [+jot.html.comments+] — places the comment on the page
- [+jot.html.moderate+] — places the moderation info on the page
- [+jot.html.form+] — places the form on the page

Let us use these placeholders in the Learning MODx blog template to get the form, comments, moderation info, and navigation in the order that we want. Change the contents of the Learning MODx blog template to the following:

```
<!DOCTYPE html PUBLIC "-//W3C//DTD XHTML 1.1//EN"  "http://www.w3.org/
TR/xhtml11/DTD/xhtml11.dtd">
<html xmlns="http://www.w3.org/1999/xhtml" xml:lang="en">
<head>
<title>Learning Modx</title>
<meta http-equiv="Content-Type" content="text/html;
charset=iso-8859-1" />
<link rel="stylesheet" type="text/css" href="assets/templates/
learningMODx/style.css" />
</head>
<body>
<div id="banner">
<h1>Learning MODx</h1>
```

```
</div>
<div id="wrapper">
<div id="container">
  <div id="content">
    [*pagetitle*]
    <br/>
    [*#content*]
    <br/>
    [!Jot? &placeholders=`1` & output=`0` &tplForm=`commentscustom`
&canpost=`Registered Users`!]
    <hr/>
    [+jot.html.comments+]
    [+jot.html.form+]
    <hr/>
    [+jot.html.moderate+]
  </div>
</div>
  <div class="clearing"></div>
</div> <!-- end of wrapper div -->
<div id="footer">It is fun and exciting to build websites with
                                        MODx</div></body>
</html>
```

Now, if you preview the page, you will notice that the elements of the comment functionality are in the order that we wanted. We also have the flexibility to insert any HTML between the placeholders. In the preceding case, we have just inserted a horizontal line.

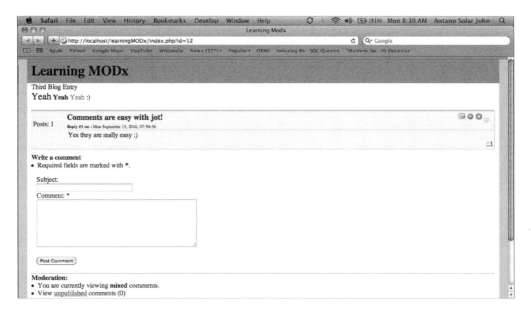

Using non-bundled snippets

Now that we have learned and discovered how to use the snippets that come bundled with MODx, let us explore how to use new snippets that are available online. For this example, we will consider one snippet called `DittoCal`. Snippet `DittoCal` allows navigation of the blog based on dates.

Installing a snippet

To install a snippet, you have to perform one or more of the following three steps:

1. Download and extract the snippet.
2. Create a snippet by using the MODx Manager interface with the available snippet code.
3. Copy the required files to the appropriate directory.

Downloading and extracting a snippet

MODx snippets can be downloaded from `http://modxcms.com/extras/`. The `DittoCal` snippet can be downloaded from `http://modxcms.com/extras/package/?package=99`. Once downloaded, you will have a ZIP file. Extract it in the same way as you extracted MODx in *Chapter 1*, *What is MODx*. Notice that although the procedure for installing most custom snippets is the same as is given here, it always helps to read the installation instructions that are available in the snippet download page, or in a ReadMe file after extracting the snippet.

Adding a snippet

Now that you have downloaded and extracted a snippet, to be able to use it, you have to create a snippet by using the MODx Manager interface. To do this, follow these steps:

1. Click on the **Manage Elements** menu item from the **Elements** menu.
2. Click on the **Snippets** tab.
3. Click on **New Snippet**.
4. Fill in the appropriate details by using the code from the extracted snippet files. For our example, it will be:

Field Name	Value
Snippet Name	DittoCal
Description	Access Posts based on dates
Snippet code	From the extracted file snippet.DittoCal.php

Note that the description is for your reference only. When you click on the **Snippets** tab, the description of the snippet that you see is taken from this field. The name that you give here is exactly what you will be using in the code when you want to call the snippet. All snippets that you download will have a file that looks similar to snippet.snippetname.php, which is a file that will contain the code to be used as the snippet code. Remember that the content area for the snippet code requires the actual code from that snippet file copied and pasted into it, and not the name of the snippet file. When you copy-paste from the snippet code, make that sure you don't get duplicate <?php...?> tags in the source. You can get by without the PHP tags; the Manager will automatically insert a set, if necessary, when saving the snippet to the database.

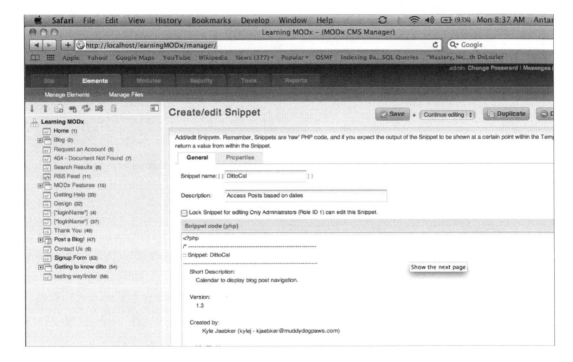

The preceding image shows the page for adding a snippet. In this page, you can give the snippet details, such as the name, description, and the snippet code itself.

Copying the required files

Some snippets that you download will have files that are required for the snippet to work, and that need to be placed in the appropriate directory. In most cases, these files will have to be placed in a specific folder within the directory `assets/snippets`, within the MODx root directory. Generally, you will have to create a folder with the snippet name inside the `assests/snippets` folder and place all of the required files there. Most snippets come with the complete folder structure when you extract them, which includes `assets/snippets/snippetname`. In such a case, you can copy the folder directly to the MODx root directory. Some snippets also have installers that do this for you. For our example snippet, we will do it as is mentioned in the `DittoCal` snippet instructions.

1. Create a folder called `DittoCal` in the `assets/snippets` directory.
2. Copy the file `JSON.php` from the extracted folder to `assets/snippets/DittoCal`.

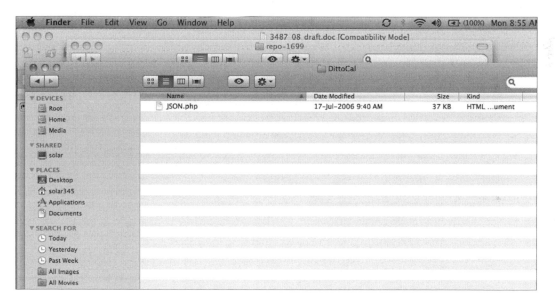

Using the snippet

The previous sections of this chapter explained how to perform research on any snippet that you may come across. For our example, we are looking at the `DittoCal` snippet. The usage of `DittoCal` is slightly different from the other snippets that we have used so far. The way to use a snippet is generally documented in the file from which you get the code for the snippet that you create. For our example, this is an excerpt from the `snippet.DittoCal.php` file.

```
/* ------------------------------------------------------------
:: Snippet: DittoCal
------------------------------------------------------------

   Short Description:
       Calendar to display blog post navigation.
   Version:
       1.3
   Created by:
     Kyle Jaebker (kylej - kjaebker@muddydogpaws.com)
   Modified by:
   Stefan Gruber                  Date: 16-Sep-07
   Mark Kaplan (modxcms.com)      Date: 18-Mar-07
   Required Usage:
       [!DittoCal?calSource=``!]

       You must create a new document with the following settings:
           template: blank
           show in menu: no
           published: yes
           searchable: no
           content type: text/plain
           document content:
           [!Ditto? &parents=`yourblogfolder` &display=`all`
&format=`json`!]

       This document is used to output your post data so that it
       can be read into the calendar.  You should set the startId
       to your blog folder and set summarize to the max number
       of posts you expect to have.  Leave everything else the same
       as above.

The documentation refers to resources as documents.
```

As you can see from the preceding text, this snippet, besides having to be called from a template or a resource, also needs a new resource to be created with a call to another snippet. We have chosen this snippet to demonstrate that each snippet has its own way of functioning, and the only way you can get to know how to use them for the functionality that you require is by reading through any documentation that is available for the snippet. In this case, it was the comments in the source code itself. Generally, all snippets will have such usage comments at the top of the code so that it is easy for those who use it to get to it. Some snippets come with well-formatted documentation that may be in the extracted folder as an .html file or .txt file, or a set of them within a docs folder. Remember—these are snippets that are created by individual users, and everyone documents their snippet in their own way. Now, let us go ahead and use the snippet in our site.

Create a resource with the following details:

Field Name	Field Value
Title	DittoCal
Content	[!Ditto? &parents=`47` &display=`all` &format=`json`!] (Replace 47 with whatever is the ID of the Post a Blog! document)
Use Template	Blank
Internet Media Type(Settings Tab)	Text/Plain
Shown in Menu	No

Edit the code of the Learning MODx default template to include the call to Dittocal:

```
<!DOCTYPE html PUBLIC "-//W3C//DTD XHTML 1.1//EN" "http://www.w3.org/
TR/xhtml11/DTD/xhtml11.dtd"> <html xmlns="http://www.w3.org/1999/
xhtml" xml:lang="en">
<head>
  <base href="[(site_url)]"></base>
  <title>Learning MODx</title>
  <meta http-equiv="Content-Type" content="text/html;
charset=iso-8859-1" />
  <link rel="stylesheet" type="text/css" href="assets/templates/
learningMODx/style.css" />
</head>
<body>
  <div id="banner">
    <h1>Learning MODx</h1>
  </div>
  <div id="wrapper">
    <div id="container">
    <div id="content">
```

```
        <div id="col-1">
        <div id="menu">
            [!Wayfinder?startId=`0` &level=`2` &outerClass=`outer`
    &innerClass='inner' &lastClass=`last` &firstClass=`first`
    &hereClass=`active`!]
        </div>
        <h1>[*pagetitle*]</h1>
        <br/>
        [*#content*]
        </div>
        <div id="col-2" >
        <div > [!WebLogin!] </div>
          <div>
          [!Ditto? &parents=`47` &tpl=`dittofrontpage`!]
          </div>
          <div>
          [!DittoCal?calSource=`59` !]
          </div>
        </div>
        </div>
    </div>
    <div class="clearing"> </div>
  </div> <!-- end of wrapper div -->
  <div id="footer">It is fun and exciting to build websites with
                                            MODx</div></body>
</html>
```

Notice that the value of the calSource parameter must be the ID of the document that you just created. Replace 59 with the ID of your DittoCal document.

Visit the home page and it will look like the following.

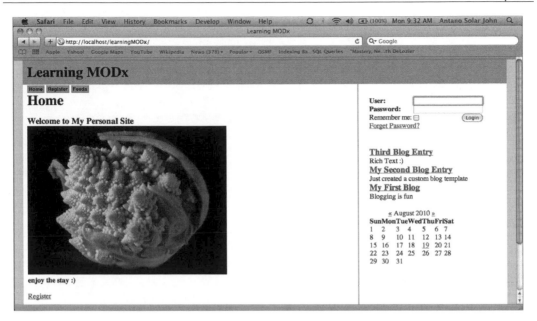

Notice the calendar below the blog posts.

Snippet without dependent files

Some snippets don't require any files. For such snippets, we don't have to perform step 3, above. An example of such a snippet is `tagcloud`.

Snippeting skills

Finding the right snippet for the right functionality is a skill in itself. There are many ways to search for the most appropriate snippet. First, you need to identify the most apt and specific words that explain what you want your snippet to do, and then you can use a search engine with those words and 'MODx'. You should also search in the MODx forums, as mentioned in *Chapter 2, Getting Started*. Finally, you can browse through the MODx extras page. If you are not able to find what you are looking for, you can also ask in the forums.

Summary

In this chapter, we have learned how to use the hundreds of snippets available in detail. We have also learned how to search for snippets that do not come packaged with MODx, and how to use them. Along the way, we have added the functionality to post comments and to navigate posts via their posting date.

9
PHx

So far in this book, we have learned how to develop our MODx site by using templates, resources, and chunks, along with snippets. Snippets provide the power of having decisions made and interacting with the databases. In short, the logical component is abstracted to the snippet, whereas the resources, templates, and chunks provide a way to show the content returned by a snippet, or the contents of a variable. In some cases, it may be necessary to perform simple conditional checks within the resources, or templates themselves. **PHx — Place Holders extended —** is a set of notations that makes this possible by adding a logic layer directly to the placeholder. PHx also makes it possible to format the output, for example by converting a string to uppercase, and so on. In this chapter, we will learn how to use this notation.

PHx in action

Let us learn how to use PHx by building a new functionality for our site that lets us add profiles of our family members and friends. We will add a new page called **Family and Friends** that will display a list of all of the individuals that we add. Once the user clicks on an individual, the site will show certain details such as the individual's name, their relationship with you, their occupation, their website, and so on. This is easy to implement; all that we have to do is to create the template variables for each of the fields, and create a template that uses these template variables. So, to display the Occupation, the template will have a code similar to the following:

```
Occupation: [*occupation*]
```

Although this might appear to work initially, there is a small glitch. When we are entering the personal details of an individual, we may not want to enter all values for every individual. In the case of not having a value for the variable, it looks cleaner to not show the label at all instead of leaving it blank. In our case, if we have no value for an occupation, it will look cleaner to not show the label **Occupation**. So here comes a need for displaying certain text only if the template variable — in this case, occupation — has a value. We can do this by using PHx without having to write a snippet.

Installing PHx

To download PHx, use the following steps:

1. Download PHx from `http://modxcms.com/extras/package/?package=342`.

2. Extract the contents of the downloaded file.

3. Create a directory called `phx` in the `assets/plugins` folder of your MODx root.

4. Copy all of the files within the extracted folder to the `assets/plugins/phx` folder. (You can also use the **Manage Files** from the **Elements** menu, if you find it easier).

5. Create a new plugin using the MODx Manager interface:

   a. Click on the **Manage Elements** menu item in the **Elements** menu

   b. Click on the **Plugins** tab

   c. Click on the **New Plugin** link

   d. Fill it with the following details:

Field Name	Field Value
Plugin Name	PHx
Plugin Code	Contents of the file `phx.plugin.txt` in the extracted folder
In System Events | OnParseDocument	Selected

6. Click on the **Save** button

Adding Family and Friends resources

Let us create a page that lists all of the members from the Family or Friends group. This resource will be a container that will have a resource for each member that you would like to add. Hence, just as you have learned earlier, a call to the `Ditto` snippet can get you all of the resources that a container holds.

1. Create a resource with the following details:

Field Name	Field Value
Title	Family and Friends
Uses template	Learning MODx default template

Code	```<ul>```
	    ```[!Ditto? &parents=`[*id]``
	```&tpl=`familyandfriendslist`!]```
	```</ul>```

`[*id*]` will be the ID of the created resource. We give the ID of this resource here as we will be adding the other resources as child resources of this resource.

2. In the above `Ditto` call, we have indicated that we are using a custom chunk to control the appearance of the listing. Create a chunk with the following details. This chunk will show a neat list of the resources that represent a member with the title and a link to the resource.

Field Name	Field Value
Chunk name	familyandfriendslist
Existing Category	Learning MODx

Chunk Code	```<li>```
	```<h3><a href="[~[+id+]~]">[+title+]</a></h3>```
	```</li>```

3. We will have to create a new template for the resources that represent the members that you add as family or friends. The template will show the various details of the member. To hold the various details of the members, we will need to create the appropriate template variables that the template can use. Create the following template variables with the given attributes, after finishing step 5:

Field Name	Field Value
Variable Name	occupation
Input Type	Text
Template Access	Family and Friends
Existing Category	Learning MODx

Field Name	Field Value
Variable Name	relationship
Input Type	Text
Template Access	Family and Friends
Existing Category	Learning MODx

Field Name	Field Value
Variable Name	website
Input Type	URL
Template Access	Family and Friends
Existing Category	Learning MODx

4. Let us create the template that the resources representing members will use. Create a template with the following details. The highlighted section of the code represents the portion that introduces the situation discussed at the beginning of this chapter. Even if the template variable has no value, there is a corresponding label shown, because we have it so in the template.

Field Name	Field Value
Template name	Family and Friends
Existing Category	Learning MODx
Template Code	The following code

Template Code

```
<!DOCTYPE html PUBLIC "-//W3C//DTD XHTML 1.1//EN" "http://www.w3.org/
TR/xhtml11/DTD/xhtml11.dtd"> <html xmlns="http://www.w3.org/1999/
xhtml" xml:lang="en">
  <head>
    <title>Learning MODx</title>
    <meta http-equiv="Content-Type" content="text/html; charset=iso-
                                                  8859-1" />
    <link rel="stylesheet" type="text/css" href=" assets/templates/
learningMODx/style.css" />
  </head>
  <body>
    <div id="banner">
      <h1>Learning MODx</h1>
    </div>

    <div id="wrapper">
```

```
            <div id="container">
              <div id="content">
                <div id="col-1">
<div id="menu">
[!Wayfinder?startId=`0` &amp;level=`2` &amp;outerClass=`outer`
&amp;innerClass='inner' &amp;lastClass=`last` &amp;firstClass=`first`
&amp;hereClass=`active`!]
</div>
                  <h1>[*pagetitle*]</h1>
                  <br/>
<table>
<tr> <td> Relationship: </td> <td> [*relationship*] </td> </tr>
<tr> <td> Occupation: </td> <td>  [*occupation*] </td> </tr>
<tr> <td> Website: </td> <td>  [*website*] </td> </tr>
</table>

<br/>

[*#content*]

      </div>

      <div id="col-2" >

      <div > [!WebLogin!] </div>

        <div>
          [!Ditto? &parents=`47` &tpl=`dittofrontpage`!]
        </div>

         </div>

      </div>

         </div>
       <div class="clearing"> </div>
    </div> <!-- end of wrapper div -->
    <div id="footer">It is fun and exciting to build websites with
                                   MODx</div></body>
</html>
```

Now that we have the template for Family and Friends, let us create a few resources that represent members. We will use these resources to observe the transformations in the appearance as we proceed.

Field Name	Field Value
Title	Richard Stallman
Uses Template	Family and Friends
Show in menu	Not selected
Resource parent	Family and Friends
Resource content	Richard Stallman is the founder of FSF, and GNU Emacs!
relationship	Friend
occupation	Geek
website	`http://www.stallman.org`

Field Name	Field Value
Title	Richard Bandler
Uses Template	Family and Friends
Show in menu	Not selected
Resource parent	Family and Friends
Resource content	Founder of Neuro Linguistic Programming (NLP)
relationship	Friend
occupation	
website	`http://www.richardbandler.com`

Preview the **Family and Friends** document and you should see a screen similar to the following screenshot:

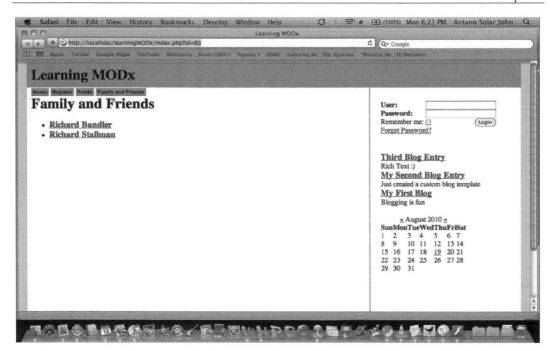

Now click on the names and you will see the following screens:

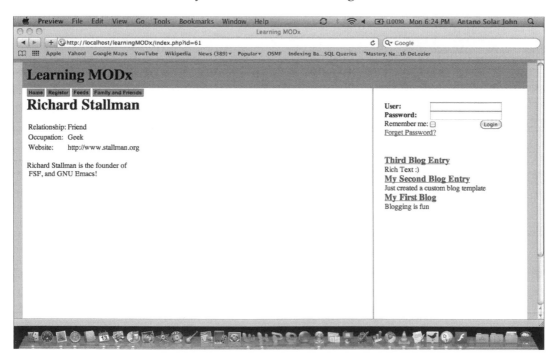

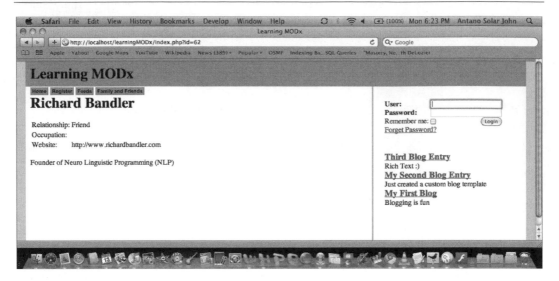

Notice that the **Occupation** field in the preceding screenshot has been left blank. This does not look clean. We will go ahead and fix this by amending the Family and Friends template to include the highlighted segment of code:

```
<!DOCTYPE html PUBLIC "-//W3C//DTD XHTML 1.1//EN" "http://www.w3.org/
TR/xhtml11/DTD/xhtml11.dtd"> <html xmlns="http://www.w3.org/1999/
xhtml" xml:lang="en">
  <head>
    <title>Learning MODx</title>
    <meta http-equiv="Content-Type" content="text/html; charset=iso-
                                                            8859-1" />
    <link rel="stylesheet" type="text/css" href="assets/templates/
learningMODx/style.css" />
  </head>
  <body>
    <div id="banner">
      <h1>Learning MODx</h1>
    </div>
    <div id="wrapper">
      <div id="container">
        <div id="content">
          <div id="col-1">
<div id="menu">
[!Wayfinder?startId=`0` &amp;level=`2` &amp;outerClass=`outer`
&amp;innerClass='inner' &amp;lastClass=`last` &amp;firstClass=`first`
&amp;hereClass=`active`!]
</div>
        <h1>[*pagetitle*]</h1>
```

```
        <br/>
<table>
<tr> <td> Relationship: </td> <td> [*relationship*] </td> </tr>
[+phx:if=`[*occupation*]`:is=``:then=``:else=`<tr> <td> Occupation:
                        </td> <td>  [*occupation*] </td> </tr>`+]
<tr> <td> Website: </td> <td>  [*website*] </td> </tr>
</table>
<br/>
[*#content*]
          </div>
      <div id="col-2" >
        <div > [!WebLogin!]  </div>
            <div>
               [!Ditto? &parents=`47` &tpl=`dittofrontpage`!]
            </div>
      </div>
        </div>
       </div>
       <div class="clearing"> </div>
     </div> <!-- end of wrapper div -->
     <div id="footer">It is fun and exciting to build websites with
                                            MODx</div>
</body>
</html>
```

Now preview the second test document again:

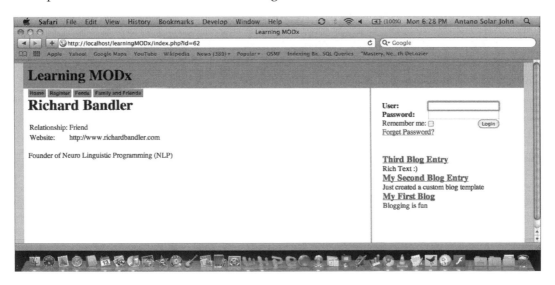

Notice that the label **Occupation** has disappeared. We still have to make sure that it is appearing in the other test resource, as Richard Stallman does have a value in the occupation field.

The preview of the first test document is as follows:

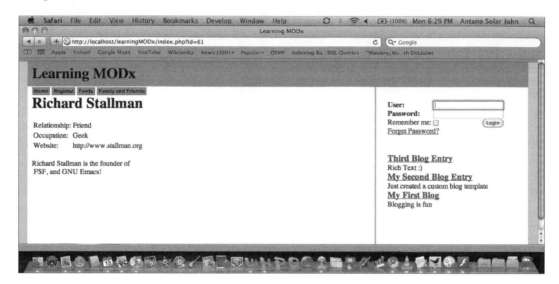

Now that we have learned how to hide the labels when the corresponding template variables are empty, we can continue to do the same for the rest of the template variables. Modify the template code to look like the following:

```
<!DOCTYPE html PUBLIC "-//W3C//DTD XHTML 1.1//EN" "http://www.w3.org/
TR/xhtml11/DTD/xhtml11.dtd"> <html xmlns="http://www.w3.org/1999/
xhtml" xml:lang="en">
  <head>
    <title>Learning MODx</title>
    <meta http-equiv="Content-Type" content="text/html; charset=iso-
                                              8859-1" />
    <link rel="stylesheet" type="text/css" href="assets/templates/
learningMODx/style.css" />
  </head>
  <body>
    <div id="banner">
      <h1>Learning MODx</h1>
    </div>
    <div id="wrapper">
      <div id="container">
        <div id="content">
```

```
            <div id="col-1">
<div id="menu">
[!Wayfinder?startId=`0`  &amp;level=`2`  &amp;outerClass=`outer`
&amp;innerClass='inner'  &amp;lastClass=`last`  &amp;firstClass=`first`
&amp;hereClass=`active`!]
</div>
        <h1>[*pagetitle*]</h1>
        <br/>
<table>
[+phx:if=`[*relationship*]`:is=``:then=``:else=`<tr> <td>
 Relationship: </td> <td> [*relationship*] </td> </tr>`+]
[+phx:if=`[*occupation*]`:is=``:then=``:else=`<tr> <td> Occupation:
                      </td> <td>  [*occupation*] </td> </tr>`+]
[+phx:if=`[*website*]`:is=``:then=``:else=`<tr> <td> Website: </td>
                      <td>  [*website*] </td> </tr>`+]
</table>
<br/>
[*#content*]
        </div>
    <div id="col-2" >
      <div > [!WebLogin!]   </div>
            <div>
               [!Ditto? &parents=`47` &tpl=`dittofrontpage`!]
            </div>
      </div>

        </div>
      </div>
      <div class="clearing"> </div>
    </div> <!-- end of wrapper div -->
    <div id="footer">It is fun and exciting to build websites with
                              MODx</div></body>
</html>
```

Now take a moment to analyze the format of the highlighted code. The notation is quite intuitive. The next section explains this notation in detail.

The PHx notation

Now that we have discovered situations in which PHx becomes helpful, we will learn the PHx syntax.

Simple usage

PHx can be used to format any template variable by using a simple syntax. The syntax is generally like this: `[+templatevariablename:modifier+]`. You can use the `[+ +]` syntax, or the `[* *]`, syntax just like you do for any other template variable.

Modifiers are special keywords that transform the value of the template variable. We have modifiers to change a string to uppercase, to lowercase, the first character to uppercase, and so on.

For example: If we have a template variable `Occupation` with the value `business`, then `[+occupation:ucfirst+]` will return `Business`.

The following is a list of the most commonly used modifiers:

- `lcase` — returns the current value with all of the alphabetic characters converted to lowercase. For example:
    - If `[+occupation+]` outputs `Engineer`, then `[+occupation:lcase+]` will output `engineer`

- `ucase` — returns the current value with all of the alphabetic characters converted to uppercase. For example:
    - If `[+occupation+]` outputs `Engineer`, then `[+occupation:ucase+]` will output `ENGINEER`

- `ucfirst` — returns the current value with the first character as uppercase. For example:
    - If `[+occupation+]` outputs `engineer`, then `[+occupation:ucfirst+]` will output `Engineer`

- `len` — returns the length of the current value. For example:
    - If `[+occupation+]` outputs `engineer`, then `[+occupation:len+]` will output `8`.

- `select=`options`` — options like `value1=output1&value2=output2`

Notice that the last modifier accepts a value after the `=` sign. The `select` modifier accepts values in the format (`value1=output1&value2=output2`) after the `=` sign. For example, if you would like to output one, two, or three instead of 1, 2, or 3 when the template variable could have the values 1, 2, or 3, you will do this by using the `select` modifier as shown in the following line of code:

```
[+templatevariablename:select=`1=one&2=two&3=three`+]
```

For a complete list of the modifiers, you can refer to the MODx wiki (`http://wiki.MODxcms.com/index.php/PHx`).

Conditional statements

Besides the above-listed modifiers that format the given template variable, we can also have conditional statements that perform an action based on a decision. The general structure of a conditional statement is as follows:

```
[+templatevariablename:condition:then=`template`:else=`template`+]
```

Here, `template` can be simple HTML or a chunk name, or even a snippet.

Conditions are of the form:

```
conditional operator = `value`
```

An example of a condition is:

```
:is=`1`
```

An example of a conditional statement is:

```
[+flag:is=`1`:then=`onchunk`:else=`offchunk`+]
```

The following is a list of the different conditional operators and their meanings:

- `is` — is equal to
- `ne` — is not equal to
- `eg` — is equal or greater than
- `el` — is equal or lower than
- `gt` — is greater than
- `lt` — is lower than
- `mo=`Webgroups`` — is the current logged in user a member of any of the given list of webgroups? The list of webgroups is separated by commas.

With these conditions, you can check if a template variable is equal to or greater than some value and similar other things, and then display a specific chunk if it is and another one if it is not.

Using the PHx placeholder

For some expressions, we may want to make use of a dummy placeholder instead of a template variable. We will now look into such examples.

Say, we are using PHx to display the username of the current logged in user. To do this, we will use the userinfo modifier. We have already learned that modifiers are used on template variables or placeholders. In the case of this modifier, we don't have to explicitly mention the placeholder, as userinfo can act only on the placeholder that stores the user's ID. In such situations, we will use the dummy placeholder, phx.

For example:

```
[+phx:userinfo=`username`+]
```

Another example is the mo operation. mo allows us to check if the currently logged in user is a member of any of the given webgroups. Again, here we are acting based on the logged in user's ID. Hence we will need to use the dummy placeholder PHx.

For example:

```
[+phx:mo=`friends`: then=`You belong to the friends group`:else=`You
                        do not belong to the friends group`+]
```

There are two other situations where you would use the phx placeholder:

- **Multiple Conditions**: This is where you want to make a decision based on one or more conditions. Multiple conditions are explained in the next subsection of this chapter.

- When using the required placeholder in more than one place in the expression:

  ```
  [+phx:if=`[*occupation*]`:is=``:then=``:else=`<tr> <td>
  Occupation: </td> <td>  [*occupation*] </td> </tr>`+]
  ```

Notice that the template variable [*occupation*] is used in the condition and in the output. Use of the if keyword is explained in the next subsection of this chapter.

Multiple conditions

To be able to use multiple conditions, you must first know how to use the if keyword. We have learned how to check the template variable for a given condition. However, how do we do the same when we use the dummy placeholder phx? We need to have a syntax to specify which template variable we are evaluating, in order to test the given condition. We can do this with the following syntax:

```
:if=`*templatevariable*`
```

After the `if` keyword followed by the template variable, the syntax remains the same. You still have to write a condition, and specify what to show if the condition is true and what to show if the condition is not. When using this syntax, multiple conditions are easy. All you need to do is use `:and` or `:or` and specify a new condition. When using `:or`, the entire expression is true if any one of the conditions is true. When using `:and`, the entire expression is true only if all of the conditions are true.

For example:

```
[+phx:if=`[*id*]`:is=`2`:or:is=`3`:then=`{ {Chunk} }`:else=`{
{OtherChunk} }`+]
```

The preceding example is from the PHx wiki documentation:
`http://wiki.modxcms.com/index.php/PHx`.

Summary

In this chapter, we have learned how to format the values in template variables, and have also seen how to make conditional decisions based on the value of template variables, and accordingly present a different output either from the HTML in the expression or from a chunk or snippet. We have also, in the process of learning PHx, added a **Family and Friends** section to the site, which allows us to hide labels when the corresponding values are empty.

10
Simple Recipes

In the previous chapters, we have learned the core concepts that are necessary for building a site using MODx. In this chapter, we will use what we have already learned to study how certain commonly-required functionalities can be implemented. We will learn how to integrate a forum, include an image gallery, develop forms that can send mail, create web user profiles, and identify similar posts for blogs.

Forums

Forums are discussion boards that allow a user to post information about a topic. Following a post, users can reply to the post, and hence create a threaded discussion. Forums are generally used for discussions. In a MODx site, one simple method to implement a forum is by using the SMF module. **SMF** is an open source community forum software application that can be installed independently of MODx. The SMF module for MODx allows the integration of MODx with SMF. This allows a user to log in to the MODx site and use the SMF forum as well, which means that your site can be powered by MODx, and can take advantage of the forum-specific functionalities of third-party software. We will see how the SMF modules make this possible. The following are the steps to get SMF working with MODx.

1. Install SMF
2. Install the SMF module for MODx

Installing SMF

As mentioned earlier, SMF is forum-specific software that we are going to use with MODx. So we will have to download and install SMF independently.

1. Download SMF from `http://download.simplemachines.org/index.php?thanks;filename=smf_1-1-11_install.zip`.

2. Extract the contents of the archive to a folder called `forum`.

3. Copy the `forum` folder to the root of the MODx installation.

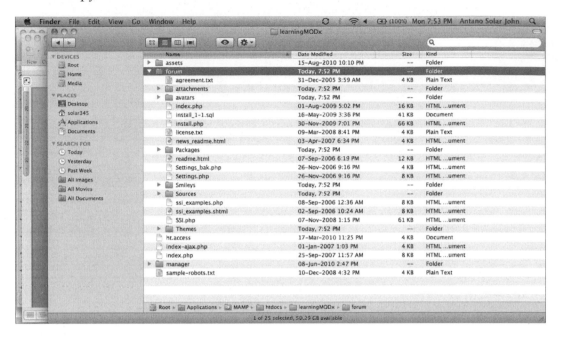

4. Visit the MODx site that we have been developing, by suffixing `/forum` at the end. For example, `http://localhost/learningMODx/forum`.

If you see something like the following screenshot, then you must change the permissions on the folders and their contents to provide the web server with **read** and **write** permissions. More information on permission issues has been given in *Chapter 2, Getting Started*.

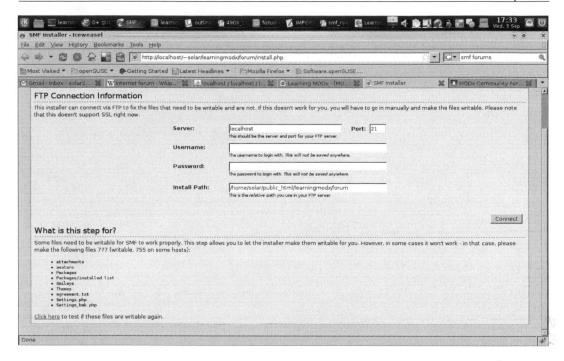

5. You will see something like the example shown in the following screenshot:

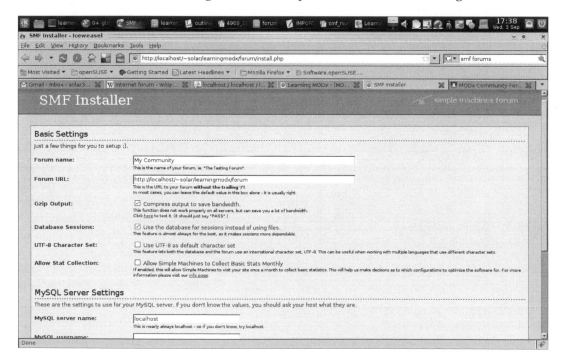

Change the following details:

Field Name	Field Value
Forum Name	Learning MODx Forum
Forum URL	The MODx site path suffixed with `/forum`;
	for example, `http://localhost/learningMODx/forum`.
MySQL username	Whatever you gave for the MODx installation (Chapter 1).
MySQL password	Whatever you gave for the MODx installation (Chapter 1).

If the given MYSQL username and password do not have permission to create a new database, then you will have to create the database yourself (Refer to *Chapter 1, What is MODx?*).

You should now see a screenshot like the following:

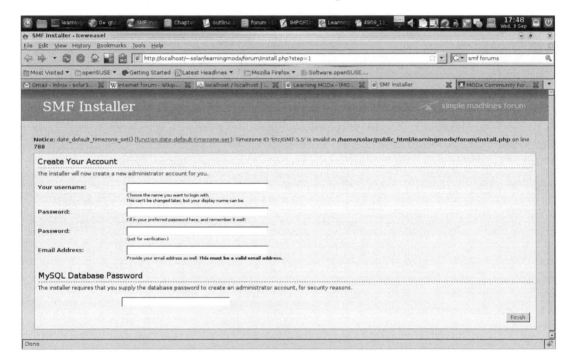

6. Fill in the following details, and then click on **Next**.

Field Name	Field Value
Your username	Any username that you will use to administer the forum. For this example, you may want to use admin.
Password	Password for the above user. For this example, give the same password as you gave for the MODx admin user.
MySQL Database Password	The MySQL password that you gave on the previous screen.

If everything went fine, you should see a page similar to the one shown in the following screenshot:

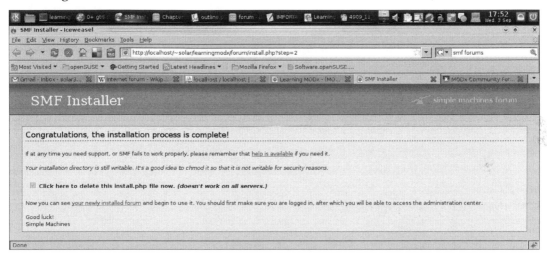

7. Click on the newly-installed forum link to see what the forum looks like (you may want to select the option that deletes the installation folder, for security reasons):

Installing the SMF module

Now that we have a working installation of SMF, we need to install the SMF module for MODx, in order to integrate MODx with SMF.

1. Download the SMF module from the MODx repository (`http://modxcms.com/extras/package/?package=419`).

2. Extract the downloaded file.

3. Copy the `install` folder to the MODx root directory.

4. Copy the contents of the `asset` folder to the `asset` folder in the MODx root directory.

5. Open the MODx URL, with a suffix of `/install` (for example: `http://localhost/learningMODx/install/`).

6. Click on **Next** on the screen that you see after opening the preceding URL.

7. With the checkbox selected for the module and the plugin, click on **Install Now**.

8. After the installation is complete, go to the manager screen in MODx.

9. Click on the **Manage Modules** menu item in the **Modules** menu.

10. Click on **SMF Connector**, and then click on the **Configuration** tab.

11. Fill in the following values:

Field Name	Field Value
CMS base URL	The base URL of the site after the domain name—for example: /learningMODx/
Forum base path	The full path of the SMF installation—for example: /var/www/learningMODx/forum
Admin User	The admin username for the forum—in our example, *admin*
Admin password	The admin password for the forum that you created when installing SMF
Login page	1
Logout page	1

12. Click on the **Save** button.

13. Click on the **SMF Connector** menu item in the **Modules** menu.

14. Click on **Synchronize Users**, and then click **OK** when asked if you really want to synchronize. If everything goes well, you will see something like the example shown in the following screenshot:

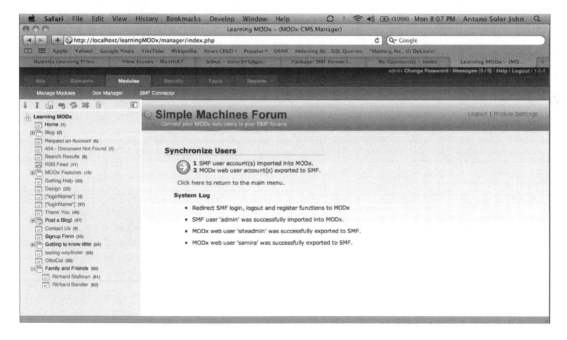

"Synchronize Users" means that the users that you have added in MODx are also created as users in SMF. Now that you have synchronized user accounts, you can test them. Log out of MODx, and log in as the user that we created earlier: **samira**. Now open the forum URL, which is, in our installation, the MODx site URL suffixed with /forum (for example, `http://localhost/learningMODx/forum`). The screen should look like the example shown in the following screenshot:

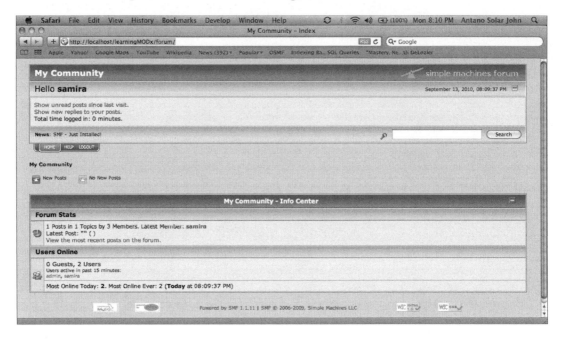

Notice that the screen says **Hello samira**, and that the user didn't have to log in again. Hence we have successfully integrated MODx with a forum application.

Note that it may be necessary to give SMF the same look and feel as the rest of your site, for which you will have to theme SMF. We will not discuss theming SMF in this book.

Image gallery

MODx has many sophisticated image gallery snippets that allow you to create an image gallery anywhere in the site. For this example, we will be using the `MaxiGallery` snippet. To get the image gallery working, install the snippet as explained in the chapter on snippets.

1. Download the snippet from the MODx repository at `http://modxcms.com/extras/package/?package=259`.

2. Extract the snippet.

3. Create a new snippet with the name `MaxiGallery`, and specify the contents of `maxigallery.txt` as the snippet code.

4. Copy the contents of the `assets` folder within the extracted folder to the `assets` folder in the root of the MODx installation. Note that it contains two folders that are to be copied:

    ° `assets/galleries` (Make sure that `assets/galleries` has write permissions)

    ° `assets/snippets/maxigallery`

5. To test the snippet, create a resource with the following details:

Field Name	Field Value
Title	Gallery
Uses template	Learning MODx default template
Document content	`[!MaxiGallery!]`

6. Preview the page and you will see something like the example shown in the following screenshot; note the **Manage pictures** button where the snippet code was placed:

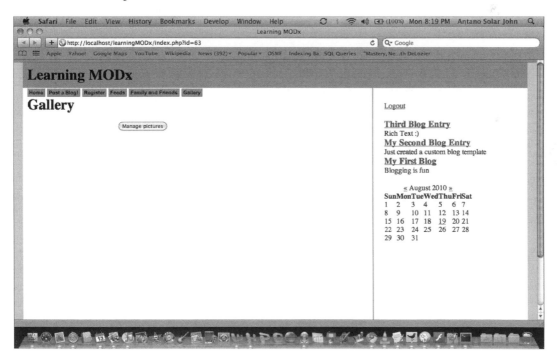

7. When you click on **Manage Pictures**, you will see something like the example shown in the following screenshot:

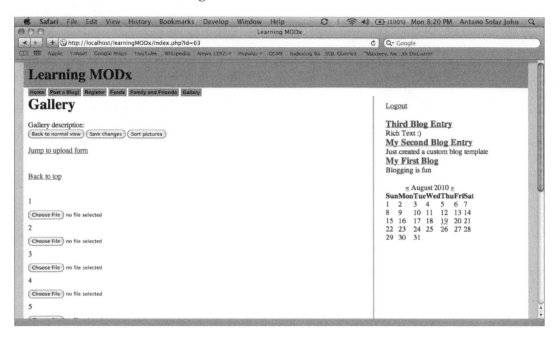

If instead you see the following error:

« MODx Parse Error »

MODx encountered the following error while attempting to parse the requested resource:

« PHP Parse Error »

PHP error debug

Error: Function split() is deprecated

then you will have to change `assets/snippets/maxigallery/maxigallery.class.inc.php` line 242

from `$sizes = split('x', $max_thumb_size);`

to `$sizes = explode('x', $max_thumb_size);`

8. Select a couple of photos by using the **Browse...** button, and then click on **Upload**. Then click on **Save changes** and then click on **Back to normal view**. You will see something like the example shown in the following screenshot:

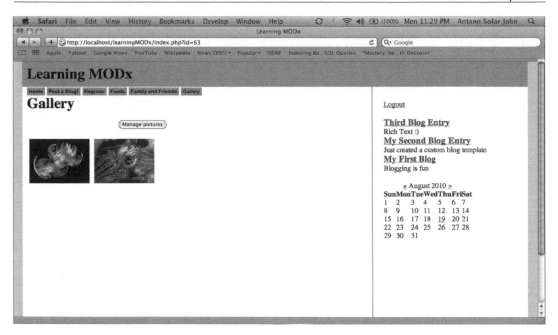

9. When you click on any of the photos, you will see something like the example shown in the following screenshot:

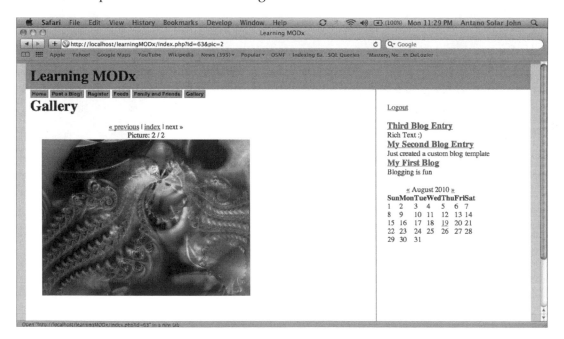

[Note that the **Manage pictures** button appears only when you have logged into the Manager as an admin, or if the web user group that the currently logged in user belongs to has edit permissions on the document.]

We have successfully created an image gallery. However, that's not all; `MaxiGallery` gives us even more flexibility. For example, you can try the following as the resource content:

```
[!MaxiGallery? &display=`embedded` &embedtype=`slimbox` !]
```

Now notice how the screen looks when you click on any of the pictures:

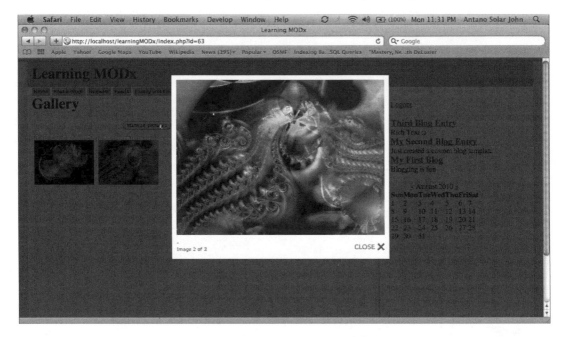

As you can see, the way that the gallery is presented now is much better than just placing images in a document. Similarly, you can add many more effects, and completely customize the way that `MaxiGallery` displays the gallery, by using its parameters and placeholders. For more information on learning how to customize a snippet, read *Chapter 8, Snippets*. What we have shown here is just the beginning; you can combine multiple snippets to come up with interesting ideas and solutions. A popular example is using `MaxiGallery` and `jot` for photo blogging. Going through each scenario and presenting the solution would be beyond the scope of this book, but this chapter intends to get you started with learning to find creative solutions yourself.

E-mailing from forms

In this section, we will discuss how to create HTML forms in MODx that can send mail to the moderator of the site. Such forms are often used as enquiry forms or feedback forms. When a user enters some information, the moderator receives an e-mail with the details. In MODx, you can achieve this by using the eForm snippet. eForm can also validate the form before sending out the e-mail. The eForm snippet comes bundled with MODx and hence you don't have to install it.

To start using eForm, let us create a resource with the following details.

Field Name	Field Value
Title	Enquiry Form
Uses template	Learning MODx default template
Document content	[!eForm? &formid=`EnquiryForm` &subject=`[+subject+]` &to=`youremailid` &tpl=`EnquiryForm` &gotoid=`1` !]

Now, create a chunk with the name EnquiryForm, and with the following content.

```
<p class="error">[+validationmessage+]</p>
<form id="EnquiryForm"
method="post" action="[~[*id*]~]" >
  <fieldset>
      <h3> Enquiry Form</h3>
            Your name:
      <p><input name="name"
                id="Name" class="text"
                type="text"
                eform="Your Name::1:" /></p></label>
      Your Email Address:
      <p><input name="email"
                id="Email"
                class="text"
                type="text"
                eform="Email Address:email:1" /></p> </label>
       Subject:
      <p><input name="subject"
                id="Subject"
                class="text"
                type="text"
                eform="Subject::1" /></p> </label>
       Enquiry:
      <p><textarea name="enquiry"
                  id="enquiry"
```

```
                eform="Enquiry:textarea:1"></textarea></p>
        </label>
        <p><input type="submit"
                class="button"
                value="Enquire Now" /></p>
    </fieldset>
</form>
```

Now preview the document and you will see something like the example shown in the following screenshot:

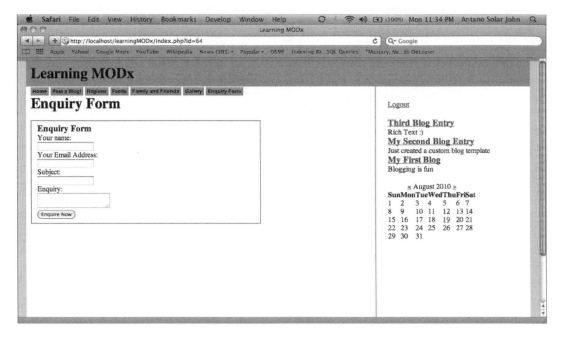

If you fill in the form and click on **Enquire Now**, it sends the user to the Home Page, and an e-mail is sent to the ID that you have given in the snippet call. If you see a page like the one shown in the following screenshot then, it means that MODx is not configured to use your mailing system. Refer to *Chapter 1, What is MODx?* to fix this.

You should also note that the form comes with validation. Try submitting the empty form and you will see something like the example shown in the following screenshot:

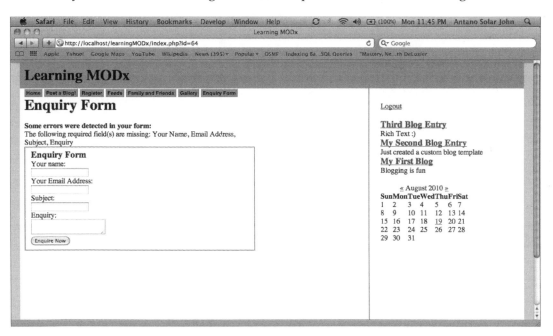

To understand what is happening, let us study the eForm snippet call:

```
[!eForm? &formid=`EnquiryForm` &subject=`[+subject+]` &to=
        `youremailid` &tpl=`EnquiryForm` &gotoid=`1` !]
```

We are making a call to eForm with various parameters, each of which is explained as follows:

- &to—the person to whom the e-mail has to be sent. If this parameter is omitted, the default emailsender, as specified in the site configuration, will be used.
- &gotoid—which page has to be shown after sending the mail.
- &subject—what field in the form has to be used as the subject for the mail.
- &tpl—which chunk will be used as the form.
- &formid—it is possible to have multiple eForms in a same page, so each form tag should have an id attribute.

Now let us have a look at the chunk code one piece at a time.

```
<form id="EnquiryForm"
method="post" action="[~[*id*]~]" >
```

The id attribute in the form tag is necessary to identify the form as related to the previous eForm snippet call. As mentioned in the explanation for the &formid parameter, this attribute takes a value that must be the same as the one given in the &formid parameter.

```
<p><input name="name"
          id="Name"
          class="text"
          type="text"
          eform="Your Name::1:" /></p></label>
```

eForm forms are like any regular HTML forms; the only difference is that every field can use the eform attribute for validation. The eform attribute takes values in the following format:

```
eform="[description/title]:[datatype]:[required]:[validation
                                  message]:[validation rule]"
```

The description/title you mention here is what will be shown as any validation message for that field.

Note that all of the preceding elements shown are optional and are separated by a colon (:). For the previous input name field we have given eform the value Your Name::1:. The interpretation of this according to the format described previously—separated by colons (:)— means that Your Name is the description/ title, there is no specified datatype, the 1 after the second colon denotes that this is a required or compulsory field, and there is no custom validation message nor any custom validation rule.

There are different kinds of `datatype`, allowing for easy validation of the commonly-used data types. The available list is:

- `string`—no specific validation other than checking to see if it's empty, and if the field is required
- `date`—checks if it is a valid date
- `integer`—checks if it is an integer
- `float`—checks if it is a number
- `email`—checks if it's a valid e-mail address
- `file`—checks if a size error occurs, but does not currently check the file type
- `html`—same as `string` except that it converts the line endings (\n) to <br /> tags

The `required` option tells `eform` whether the field is a required field or not. For the `name` field, you can see that we have mentioned one indicating that it is a required field. `validation message` can be any message that you want to show when the field is empty and required, or the field value is not of the given data type or doesn't fit into the validation rules. Finally, in addition to the given data types, you can also write custom validation rules. You can find more information on e-forms in the MODx wiki at `http://wiki.MODxcms.com/index.php/EForm`.

User profiles

MODx allows us to implement user profiles by using the `WebLoginPE` snippet. In this section, we will be using the `WebLoginPE` snippet to list the users, view their profile, and edit one's own profile.

Installing WebLoginPE

`WebLoginPE` has a nice support site. You may want to look at `http://sottwell.com/assets/snippets/webloginpe/docs/index.html`.

1. Download the snippet from the MODx repository at `http://modxcms.com/extras/package/?package=495`.
2. Extract the snippet.
3. Create a folder named `webloginpe` in the `assets/snippets` folder, in the root directory of the MODx installation.
4. Copy all of the files from the extracted folder to the folder `assets/snippets/webloginpe`.

5. Create a new snippet by using the MODx Manager, with the name `WebLoginPE`, and using the code from `webloginpe.snippet.php` file in the extracted folder as the snippet code.

Edit profile

Now that we have `WebLoginPE` installed, let us use it.

```
[!WebLoginPE? &type=`profile`!]
```

A call to the snippet with the parameters and value as shown previously lists all of the users and allows the currently logged-in user to edit his or her profile. So let us create a resource with the following details:

Field Name	Field Value
Title	My Profile
Uses template	Learning MODx default template
Show in menu	Unchecked
Document Content	`[!WebLoginPE? &type=`profile`!]`

Now, log in as **samira** into the site, and preview this page. You will see something like the example shown in the following screenshot:

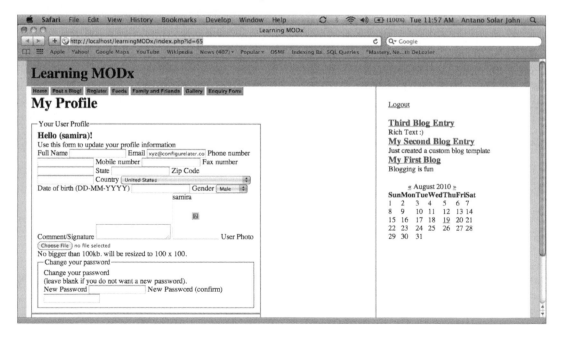

You can change some values and notice that the changes get saved and the new values are shown when you edit the profile again. The default profile edit for the user has many common fields such as the full name, e-mail ID, photo, and so on. You can also change the fields, and the look of the edit form, by using chunks. We will leave that as an exercise for the reader.

List users and view their profiles

To list the users and view their profiles, create a resource with the following details:

Field Name	Field Value
Title	Users
Uses template	Learning MODx default template
Document Content	`[!WebLoginPE? &type=`users`!]`

If you preview this page, it will look like the following screenshot, which lists all of the users of the site:

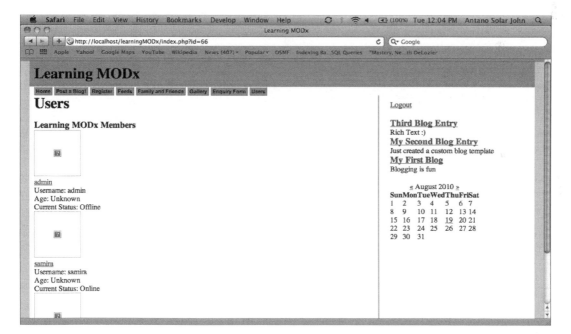

If you click on any user, it will show that user's profile, as in shown the following screen. The Profile View page also has provisions for sending a message to the user.

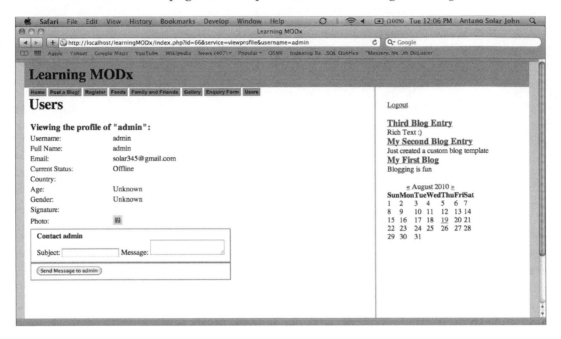

Link to edit a profile

Now you have an edited Profile page. For users to be able to access the page, we need to be able to show a link to that page. The link should only appear when the user is logged in. The snippet Personalize, which comes with MODx allows us to do this:

Edit the Learning MODx default template to add the highlighted section.

```
<!DOCTYPE html PUBLIC "-//W3C//DTD XHTML 1.1//EN" "http://www.w3.org/
TR/xhtml11/DTD/xhtml11.dtd"> <html xmlns="http://www.w3.org/1999/
xhtml" xml:lang="en">
<head>
  <base href="[(site_url)]"></base>
  <title>Learning MODx</title>
  <meta http-equiv="Content-Type" content="text/html;
charset=iso-8859-1" />
  <link rel="stylesheet" type="text/css" href="assets/templates/
learningMODx/style.css" />
</head>
<body>
  <div id="banner">
  <h1>Learning MODx</h1>
```

```
    </div>
    <div id="wrapper">
    <div id="container">
      <div id="content">
      <div id="col-1">
      <div id="menu">
        [!Wayfinder?startId=`0` &level=`2` &outerClass=`outer`
&innerClass='inner' &lastClass=`last` &firstClass=`first`
&hereClass=`active`!]
      </div>

      <h1>[*pagetitle*]</h1>
      <br/>
      [*#content*]
    </div>
    <div id="col-2" >
      <div > [!Personalize? yesChunk=`profilelink`!]
                                  [!WebLogin!]  </div>

      <div>
        [!Ditto? &parents=`47` &tpl=`dittofrontpage`!]
      </div>
      <div>
      [!DittoCal?calSource=`59` !]
      </div>
      </div>
    </div>
  </div>
  <div class="clearing"> </div>
  </div> <!-- end of wrapper div -->
  <div id="footer">It is fun and exciting to build websites with
                                  MODx</div></body>
</html>
```

What we are doing here is telling the `Personalize` snippet to render a chunk call to the `profilelink`, if the user is logged in.

Now, let us create the chunk `profilelink`, to display the link. Place the following code in the new chunk:

```
<a href="[~65~]">My Profile</a>
```

Replace 65 with the document ID of your My Profile document.

Now the Front Page, if you are logged in, looks like the example shown in the following screenshot:

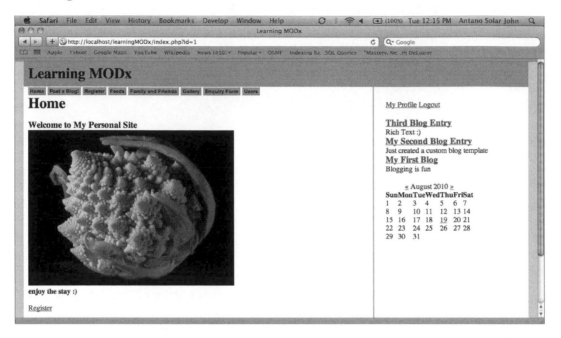

Notice that the link does not appear when you are logged out.

There are many ways to have user profiles in MODx; what we have shown here, using `WebLoginPE`, is just one of the ways. The other possibilities include associating every new user with a resource, and assigning those resources with a template that has the template variables necessary to store the user's data.

Similar posts

It would be nice to show the similar posts from a category when displaying blog entries. At first thought, it may be tempting to think that we will need to look for a snippet that does this. This example will demonstrate that many functionalities can be implemented by the proper usage of the snippets that you already know. In this case, we will be using the `Ditto` snippet.

The `Ditto` call that has to be included in the `Learning MODx` blog template is:

```
[!Ditto? &parents=`47` &filter=`tvBlogcategories,[*Blogcategories*],7
                                        |id,[*id*],2`!]
```

This section will teach you, step by step, how we came to get this snippet call. It is important that you learn the process of building a complex snippet call. When the solution for the requirement is approached logically, solving one hurdle at a time, the whole procedure becomes very simple.

We already know that Ditto can be used to show all of the MODx resources from a particular container. Because all of our blogs are in a container with an ID of 47 (in an earlier chapter, we explained that this ID can be different for you), in order to display all the blogs we will call Ditto as follows:

```
[!Ditto? &parents=`47`!]
```

We have also learned that we can use filters to display resources with a specific template variable value. This has already been demonstrated when we created RSS feeds for a different categories of blogs. So a call of:

```
[!Ditto? &parents=`47` &filter=`tvBlogcategories, IT, 7`!]
```

will display all of the blogs from the IT category. Now, this is fine when we are in a blog page that is also of the IT category. However, when we are visiting a blog that is of the Sports category, we will want to display blogs from the Sports category. So in the filter, instead of IT or Sports, we will have to have a variable that changes its value depending on which resource is being viewed. Here, we can use the template variable of the resource itself to achieve this. Hence,

```
[!Ditto? &parents=`47` &filter=`tvBlogcategories, [*Blogcategories*],7
```

will translate to

```
[!Ditto? &parents=`47` &filter=`tvBlogcategories,IT,7
```

in a blog with the category as IT, and to

```
[!Ditto? &parents=`47` &filter=`tvBlogcategories,Sports,7
```

in a blog with the category as Sports.

The snippet call to show the similar posts is almost complete, as we show blogs from the same category. But there is one more enhancement that needs to be done. We don't want the blog page that we are currently displaying to be listed in the list of similar posts as well. Therefore, we need to filter out the current resource. We already know that we can club filters together by using the | operator, and also that we can filter resources based on the ID. A filtering expression like:

```
id,1,2
```

will filter out resource 1. What we need is to replace 1 with the current resource's ID. So the filter expression will be:

```
id,[*id*],2
```

By clubbing all of this together, we get:

```
[!Ditto? &parents=`47` &filter=`tvBlogcategories,[*Blogcategories*],7
|id,[*id*],2`!]
```

We can implement this by modifying the Learning MODx blog template to the contain following addition:

```
<!DOCTYPE html PUBLIC "-//W3C//DTD XHTML 1.1//EN"  "http://www.w3.org/
TR/xhtml11/DTD/xhtml11.dtd">
<html xmlns="http://www.w3.org/1999/xhtml" xml:lang="en">
<head>
<title>Learning Modx</title>
<meta http-equiv="Content-Type" content="text/html;
charset=iso-8859-1" />
<link rel="stylesheet" type="text/css" href="assets/templates/
learningMODx/style.css" />
</head>
<body>
<div id="banner">
<h1>Learning MODx</h1>
</div>
<div id="wrapper">
<div id="container">
  <div id="content">
  [*pagetitle*]
    <br/>
    [*#content*]
    <br/>
    [!Jot? &placeholders=`1` & output=`0` &tplForm=`commentscustom`
&canpost=`Registered Users`!]
    <hr/>
    [+jot.html.comments+]
    [+jot.html.form+]
    <hr/>
    [+jot.html.moderate+]

        <div id="col-2" >
        <div > [!WebLogin!]
  </div>

<div>
<h3>Similar Posts in [*blogCategories*]</h3>

[!Ditto? &parents=`47` &filter=`tvblogCategories,[*blogCategories*],7|
id,[*id*],2`!]

</div>
```

```
</div>
  <div class="clearing"></div>
</div> <!-- end of wrapper div -->
<div id="footer">It is fun and exciting to build websites with
                                      MODx</div></body>
</html>
```

Notice that we have also used the template variable [*Blogcategories*] in the caption. Now you can preview a blog and it will look like the example shown in the following screenshot, with the new **Related Posts** functionality working.

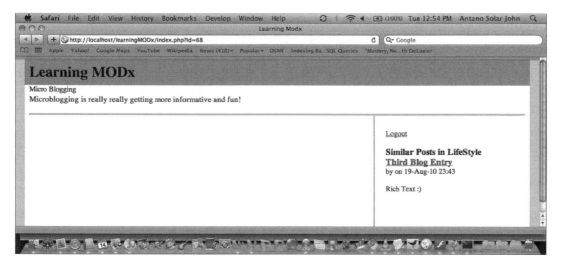

Summary

In this chapter, we have seen how we can use what we have already learned to create:

- Forums by using the SMF module
- Image galleries by using `MaxiGallery`
- Enquiry forms supporting validation, and e-mail with eForms
- User profiles by using `WebLoginPe`
- Similar posts by using Ditto

We have also seen how we can approach a given requirement logically, step by step, to construct the complex snippet calls that provide a solution. This chapter showcases everything that you have learned so far, integrated in quick demonstrations.

11
Creating Snippets

So far, we have learned how to use snippets to get the required functionality for our site. What about when there are no snippets available to do what we want to do? We might have to create the snippet ourselves. Fortunately, unlike most other CMSs, MODx requires no—or very little—overhead to turn any regular PHP code into a snippet.

 This chapter requires you to have a basic knowledge of PHP. However, even if this is not the case, I recommend that you read this chapter, as it will help you to better understand snippets.

Learning to create a snippet

In this section, we will learn to create a snippet by using a simple 'Hello World' program in PHP. To test the output, we will create a resource with the following details:

Field Name	Field Value
Title	Creating a Snippet
Uses template	Learning MODx default template
Document content	[!helloworld!]
Show in menu	Disable

From the earlier chapter on using snippets, we have learned that a snippet can do one or more of the following three things:

- Return HTML output that gets inserted in place of the snippet call
- Create and store values in placeholders, which can later be used in the document or template that called the snippet

- Create and store values in placeholders, process a chunk that uses these placeholders, and insert the chunk's HTML with the placeholders' values in the document or template that called the snippet

In this section, we will learn how to make regular PHP code do all of these things. For this demonstration, we will convert the following PHP code to behave like a snippet.

```php
<?php
  echo "Hello World!<br>";
  echo "It is a beautiful day";
?>
```

Returning output

Let us create the snippet Hello World! now.

1. Click on the **Manage Elements** menu in the **Elements** menu.
2. Click on the **Snippets** tab.
3. Click on **New Snippet** and fill in the following details:

Field Name	Field Value
Snippet name	**helloworld**
Snippet Description	**Hello World!**
Snippet code	The preceding PHP code
Existing Category in Properties tab	**Learning MODx**

4. Click on the **Save button**.

Now, preview the document that you have just created. You will see a screen similar to the one shown in the following screenshot:

The snippet works without any changes to the regular PHP code. However, this method is not recommended, as it might result in inconsistent behavior. The recommended method of rendering the output is to keep concatenating whatever has to be shown in a string and then finally return the string. Change the code in the Hello World! snippet to the following code:

```php
<?php
  $message = "Hello World!<br>";
  $message .="It is a beautiful day";
return $message;
?>
```

Now preview the resource and notice that the output has not changed and is the same as the previous screenshot. The only change is that you have used the recommended method to display the same output.

To summarize what you have just learned—whatever you finally return by using the return keyword gets shown in the place of the snippet call.

Returning placeholders

Now that we have seen how to return output in place of the snippet call, we will now learn how to create placeholders. We will also learn that the user has the flexibility to use the placeholders anywhere in the resource. What basically happens is this: we decide that we want to have a certain placeholder, we create it in the snippet and assign it a value, the placeholder is used after the snippet call in the resource, and the resource shows the value of the placeholder.

To create a placeholder and assign a value to it, we use the modx function $modx->setPlaceholder().

The function accepts two parameters—the name of the placeholder and its value. Hence, the syntax is $MODx->setPlaceholder(placeholdername, value);.

Now let us modify our snippet to use placeholders using what we have just learned.

Modify the snippet code to the following:

```php
<?php
  $modx->setPlaceholder("message1", "Hello World!");
  $modx->setPlaceholder("message2","It is a beautiful day");
  return;
?>
```

Note that we could have just created one placeholder with the name `message` and the value as `$message`. We have created two, just to demonstrate how placeholders can be placed anywhere in the document.

To test the results, we also need to modify the **Create a Snippet** resource to use the placeholders. Change the content of the MODx resource to the following:

```
[!helloworld!]
Before Placeholder1 <br>
[+message1+] <br>
Before Placeholder2 <br>
[+message2+]
```

Now preview the document, and it will look similar to the example shown in the following screenshot:

Processing a chunk

In the previous example, we had the following code in the resource:

```
Before Placeholder1 <br>
[+message1+] <br>
Before Placeholder2 <br>
[+message2+]
```

It is possible to isolate this from the resource, and hence make the code even cleaner to maintain. We can do this by placing this code in a chunk and making the snippet call this chunk. Let us try this by doing the following:

1. Change the resource code to

    ```
    [!helloworld!]
    ```

2. Create a chunk called `helloworld`, with the following content:

```
Before Placeholder1 <br>
[+message1+] <br>
Before Placeholder2 <br>
[+message2+]
```

3. Change the snippet code to the following:

```
<?php
$MODx->setPlaceholder('message1', "Hello World!");
$MODx->setPlaceholder("message2","It is a beautiful day");
$output = $MODx->getChunk("helloworld");
return $output;
?>
```

If you preview the page, it will look like the previous screenshot. What has changed is the way that we have implemented the same thing. It is cleaner and easier to maintain, by using chunks.

 This example uses only one chunk to demonstrate the concept of chunks. A snippet can use multiple chunks as well, if there is a necessity to do so.

Using parameters

Now that we have made our snippet create placeholders and then use a chunk for rendering the output, it would be nice if we could make our snippet more flexible. What if it could use any chunk, instead of a predefined `helloworld` chunk to render the output? This might be necessary if you want to call the same snippet twice on the same page, or if you want a different output or style for each call. To make this possible, we will need to be able to get the chunk name from the snippet call. This can be done by using parameters. By using parameters in a call, we can pass the snippet values that it can use. For this example, we will use a parameter called `&tpl`. The snippet will check if the call to it has any value for `tpl`. If it does, then it will use that value as the chunk name; if it doesn't exist, it will use `helloworld` as the chunk name. This way, the snippet has a sensible default value and yet provides a mechanism to override it.

To see the use of parameters, change the `helloworld` snippet code to the following:

```
<?php
$tpl = (isset($tpl))? $tpl : 'helloworld';
$modx->setPlaceholder('message1', "Hello World!");
$modx >setPlaceholder("message2","It is a beautiful day");
$output = $modx->getChunk($tpl);
```

```
    return $output;
?>
```

Notice that the parameters from the resource/template are available as regular PHP variables within the snippet. We are using a ternary operator to set the value of `$tpl` to `helloworld`, if there was no custom value passed along with the call.

Modify the document that you created earlier, which was titled `creating a snippet`, to contain the following:

```
[!helloworld?tpl=`helloworldx`!]
```

Create a new chunk called `helloworldx` with the following content:

```
This is from chunk helloworldx<br>

Before Placeholder1 <br>
[+message1+] <br>
Before Placeholder2 <br>
[+message2+]
```

Now preview the document; it will look similar to the example shown in the following screenshot:

Notice that this call to the snippet used the chunk `helloworldx` instead of the `helloworld` chunk.

MODx API

MODx provides APIs that you can use to avoid recreating commonly-used functions. The MODx APIs are accessed through the `DocumentParser` object $modx. You can explore more of the MODx internals by trying the following at the top of the `helloworld` snippet, after the `<?php` open tag:

```
echo '<pre>';
print_r($MODx);
echo '</pre>';
exit;
```

This will print the entire structure of the $modx object, so you can learn a great deal from the output.

You can use any of the available API functions from within the snippet using the `$modx->functionname()` syntax. In fact, the functions that you have been using to set the placeholders, and to display a chunk, are themselves a part of the MODx API that is available through the $modx object.

Next, we will see examples of a few of them:

*   `$modx->getDocument(1)` will get all the property and values of resource 1
*   `$modx->getAllChildren(1)` will get all of the child resources of resource 1
*   `$modx->getTemplateVars` will return an array of all of the template variables that the template for the current resource is using

DBAPI

The DBAPI is a sub-class of the `DocumentParser`. It acts as glue between the database and the PHP code in MODx. Using these functions instead of the PHP database functions will allow you to write code that doesn't have to be specific for any database. The following is a list of a few DBAPI functions. When using DBAPI, you will be using the `$table_prefix` variable, which will give the prefix to the table, including the database name. This again ensures that you don't have to worry about migration issues when moving a site that is using your snippet to another location with a new database name.

$MODx->db->select

`$MODx->db->select` can be used for executing a SQL query. All arguments, except `$from`, are optional.

Syntax: `select([string $fields [, string $from [, string $where [, string $orderby [, string $limit]]]]])`.

Parameters:

- `$fields` is the field or column name(s) that you want returned. If this is left blank, it will default to all (`*`).
- `$from` is the table to query. If this is left blank, the function will return `false`.
- `$where` is the full string of the WHERE clause of the MySQL query. Leave it blank to not perform WHERE matching.
- `$orderby`, if needed, can either be ASC or DESC.
- `$limit` is the limit of the number of results to return; leave blank for all.

For example:

```
$res = $MODx->db->select("", $table_prefix.".MODx_site_content",
                              "parent = 10", "ASC" , 10);
```

This will get ten records in ascending order that have the value 10 for the field `parent` from the table MODx_site_content.

$MODx->db->getRecordCount

`$MODx->db->getRecordCount` retrieves the number of rows from a resultset.

Syntax: `getRecordCount ($resultset)`.

Parameter:

- `$resultset`—any result set that is returned by `select` or `show`

For example:

```
$count = $MODx->db->getRecordCount($res);
```

If the resultset `$res` has five records, `$count` will be 5.

$MODx->db->makeArray

`$MODx->db->makeArray` will convert a resultset into a multidimensional array.

Syntax: `makeArray($resultset)`.

Parameters:

- `$resultset`—any resultset that is returned by the usage of `select` or `show`

For example:

```
$resultsarr = $MODx->db->makeArray($resultset);
```

`$resultarr` will contain a multidimensional array representation of the resultset.

Fortunes

Now that you have learned how to create snippets, let us create a snippet that displays a random fortune from the database. Fortunes are just quotations from famous texts. These are like a "quote of the day". They are called fortunes in the UNIX culture, after the introduction of the command-line program called *fortune*, many decades ago.

Creating the table

We will create a table that will hold the fortune and the author's name, using phpMyAdmin, to keep it simple. Most snippets that use a custom table will automatically create the table, if it doesn't exist already.

1. Open phpMyAdmin. The URL for phpMyAdmin will be different depending on your method of installation. If you choose to install Apache and PHP individually, then you will have to install phpMyAdmin first. If you are using XAMPP, as explained in *Chapter 2, Getting Started*, then the URL is `http://localhost/phpmyadmin`.

2. Log in using the username **mySQL** and the password that you created initially.

3. Click on the **learningMODx** table.

4. At the bottom of the page, under the heading **Create New Table**, name the table **modx_fortunes** and set **Number of fields** to **3**.

5. Specify the following values for the fields:

Field	Type	Length	Extra	Primary key
id	INT		**Auto Increment (In some versions of PHPmyadmin this appears as a checkbox A_I)**	Enabled
text	VARCHAR	255		
author	VARCHAR	100		

6. Insert a few fortune records, such as:

It's hard to read through a book on the principles of magic without glancing at the cover periodically to make sure it isn't a book on software design.
— Bruce Tognazzini

Debugging is twice as hard as writing the code in the first place. Therefore, if you write the code as cleverly as possible, you are, by definition, not smart enough to debug it.
— Brian Kernighan

> *No emotion, any more than a wave, can long retain its own individual form.*
> — *Henry Ward Beecher*

Code for fortunes

We now have a table with records that contain the fortunes. The following is the snippet code that displays a random fortune:

```php
<?php
$res = $modx->db->select("*", $table_prefix."MODx_fortunes"); // Fetch
all the records from the table
$count = $modx->db->getRecordCount( $res); // Get the total number of
records
if($count==0)
{
return "There are no Fortunes";
}
$x = rand(0,$count-1); // Get a random number between 0 and record
count
$fortunes = $modx->db->makeArray($res); // Convert the recordset to an
array
$fortune = $fortunes[$x]; // Get the nth record where n is the random
number
$o = '<h3>Fortune</h3>';
$o .= $fortune["text"];
$o .= "<br>";
$o .= $fortune['author'];
return $o;
?>
```

The preceding code queries the table for all the records using the MODx DBAPI, from which we get the number of records. Then a random number is generated from 0 to a count less than the number of records, and we pick the record after converting the resultset to an array, using the random number as the index. We could also have used the rand() function in the SQL query with LIMIT 1 to get a random record, but because the name of the function is different across MySQL and PostgreSQL, we would have then had to implement the database-specific code.

Now create a snippet with the following details:

Field Name	Field Value
Snippet name	Fortunes
Snippet Code	The preceding code
Existing Category	Learning MODx

Testing the snippet

Let's test the snippet by calling it from the Learning MODx default template. Modify the template code of the Learning MODx default template to:

```
<!DOCTYPE html PUBLIC "-//W3C//DTD XHTML 1.1//EN" "http://www.w3.org/
TR/xhtml11/DTD/xhtml11.dtd"> <html xmlns="http://www.w3.org/1999/
xhtml" xml:lang="en">
  <head>
    <base href="[(site_url)]"></base>
  <title>Learning MODx</title>
  <meta http-equiv="Content-Type" content="text/html;
charset=iso-8859-1" />
    <link rel="stylesheet" type="text/css" href="assets/templates/
learningMODx/style.css" />
   </head>
  <body>
    <div id="banner">
    <h1>Learning MODx</h1>
    </div>
    <div id="wrapper">
    <div id="container">
    <div id="content">
    <div id="col-1">
    <div id="menu">
        [!Wayfinder?startId=`0` &level=`2` &outerClass=`outer`
&innerClass='inner' &lastClass=`last` &firstClass=`first`
&hereClass=`active`!]
    </div>
      <h1>[*pagetitle*]</h1>
      <br/>
      [*#content*]
     </div>
     <div id="col-2" >
    <div> [!Fortunes!] </div>
    <div > [!Personalize?yesChunk=`profilelink`!]
    [!WebLogin!]   </div>
       <div>
        [!Ditto? &parents=`47` &tpl=`dittofrontpage`!]
       </div>
       <div>
       [!DittoCal?calSource=`59` !]
       </div>
      </div>
    </div>
```

```
    </div>
    <div class="clearing"> </div>
    </div> <!-- end of wrapper div -->
    <div id="footer">It is fun and exciting to build websites with
                                        MODx</div></body>
</html>
```

Now you can preview the front page and it will look similar to the following screenshot:

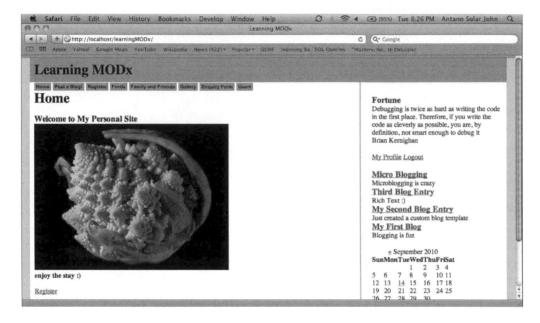

Refresh the page to see if you get another fortune.

Chunks, placeholders, and parameters

We have now got the fortune snippet working, so let us enhance it. We can perform the following improvements on it:

- Create placeholders for the fortune text and the author
- Define a parameter to specify a chunk name
- Process the output using the given chunk

We have already seen how to do all of these things in the Hello World! example.

To create placeholders:

```
$modx->setPlaceholder('fortunetext',$fortune["text"]);
$modx->setPlaceholder('fortuneauthor',$fortune["author"]);
```

To accept parameters for the output template:

```
$tpl = (isset($tpl))? $tpl : 'fortune';
```

To process the output using the given chunk:

```
$o = $modx->getChunk($tpl);
```

Hence, the final snippet of code will be:

```
<?php
  $tpl = (isset($tpl))? $tpl : 'fortunes';
  $res = $modx->db->select("*", $table_prefix."MODx_fortunes"); //
Fetch all the records from the table
  $count = $modx->db->getRecordCount( $res); // Get the total number
of records
  $x = rand(0,$count-1); // Get a random number between 0 and record
count
  $fortunes = $modx->db->makeArray($res); // Convert the recordset to
an array
  $fortune = $fortunes[$x]; // Get the nth record where n is the
random number
  $modx->setPlaceholder('fortunetext',$fortune["text"]);
  $modx->setPlaceholder('fortuneauthor',$fortune["author"]);
  $o = $modx->getChunk($tpl);
  return $o;
?>
```

Modify the Fortune snippet to contain the preceding code.

Next, you will have to create a chunk for the snippet to use. As we are not passing any parameter in the snippet call, it will use the chunk named fortunes. So let us create a chunk with the following details:

Field Name	Field Value
Chunk name	fortunes
Existing Category	Learning MODx
Chunk code	`<h3>Fortune</h3>` `[+fortunetext+]` ` ` `[+fortuneauthor+]`

Now, preview the front page again. You should be able to see the fortune, just as before.

Using files

It is also possible that you have a large snippet that you want to split into multiple files. In such a case, other files can be included from within the snippet. For example, to include a file for the fortune snippet, the line of code could be:

```
include MODX_BASE_PATH.'assets/snippets/fortunes/filename.php';
```

`MODX_BASE_PATH` stores the root directory of the installation.

The convention followed when using external files is to place them in a folder that has the same name as the snippet and that is inside the `assets/snippets folder`.

Summary

In this chapter, you have learned how to create snippets and the different ways of rendering output. You have also learned how to use the available MODx APIs as well as why you should use them. You have created a new snippet for the site to display a random fortune. The snippet accepts a parameter for a chunk and renders the output by using chunks and placeholders. You also learned how snippets can make use of external files.

12
SEO, Deployment, and Security

In this chapter, we will discuss all that you need to take care of once you have developed your site. We will discuss how MODx helps you to take your site to the top of the search ladder. After that, we will deal with deployment and keeping your site secured.

SEO

We all know that **Search Engine Optimization (SEO)** is about getting a better rank in the search engines like Google, so that your site appears towards the top of the results list when someone searches for the content that is available on your site. In this section, we will discuss the various factors that contribute to getting a site optimized for a search engine, and also discuss what MODx provides to make this possible.

 Please note that like the CTO of Google says—" ", it all comes down to what you really have. However, there are certain fundamentals that you can take care of so that you can optimize the results that you already get.

Search engine-friendly URLs

Clean URLs are URLs without the ugly `?=xxxxxxxxxx` at the end. This format is used to pass parameters to a page by appending a `?` and a key (`=`) value pair to the URL. For example, to pass `id = 7` to the `index.php` page, the URL might look like `http://localhost/learningMODx/index.php?id=7`. If you observe closely, you will notice that whatever resource you want to visit, MODx is actually calling the `index.php` page with the ID of the respective resource ID as a parameter. Almost all CMSs behave in the same way. All CMSs execute only one PHP page, which in turn parses the required resource. Friendlier URLs mean that instead of using the following URL `http://localhost/learningMODx/index.php?id=7`, we would want the URL to look like `http://localhost/learningMODx/7`. This URL appears friendlier, not just to the end users, but also to machines. If you would like to find out more about how this appears friendly to machines, you might want to Google for 'REST' and read about it. Now that this URL appears friendlier to machines, there are greater chances that it will be ranked higher. MODx supports clean URLs.

To turn on clean URLs, you must first have `mod_rewrite` loaded to Apache.

If you are using Apache with XAMPP, as explained in *Chapter 2, Getting Started*, then this feature is activated by default. Alternatively, if you are using Apache from any Debian-based distribution, you can load the module by issuing the following commands:

```
a2enmod rewrite
apache2ctl restart
```

What essentially happens, when using the `rewrite` module, is that there is a file in the MODx directory called `.htaccess` that contains rules on how to translate the URL. So although the requested URL is `http://localhost/learningMODx/7`, the `rewrite` module of Apache after reading the configuration file will translate this to `http://localhost/learningMODx/index.php?id=7`. You can also manually edit the `ht.access` file to specify new mapping rules if you like.

You will find a file with the name `ht.access` in the MODx root directory. Rename this file to `.htaccess`. Do the same thing with the `ht.access` file in the `manager` directory.

Now, open the `.htaccess` file in the MODx root directory and edit the line `RewriteBase /` to contain the `MODxfolderpath`, which, in our case, is `learningMODx`. Hence you will have to change the above line to `RewriteBase /learningMODx`. So `.htaccess` should now look like the following:

```
# For full documentation and other suggested options, please see
# http://svn.modxcms.com/docs/display/MODx096/Friendly+URL+Solutions
# including for unexpected logouts in multi-server/cloud environments
# and especially for the first three commented out rules

#php_flag register_globals Off
#AddDefaultCharset utf-8
#php_value date.timezone Europe/Moscow

Options +FollowSymlinks
RewriteEngine On
RewriteBase /learningMODx

# Fix Apache internal dummy connections from breaking [(site_url)]
cache
RewriteCond %{HTTP_USER_AGENT} ^.*internal\ dummy\ connection.*$ [NC]
RewriteRule .* - [F,L]

# Rewrite domain.com -> www.domain.com -- used with SEO Strict URLs
plugin
#RewriteCond %{HTTP_HOST} .
#RewriteCond %{HTTP_HOST} !^www\.example\.com [NC]
#RewriteRule (.*) http://www.example.com/$1 [R=301,L]

# Exclude /assets and /manager directories and images from rewrite
rules
RewriteRule ^(manager|assets)/*$ - [L]
RewriteRule \.(jpg|jpeg|png|gif|ico)$ - [L]

# For Friendly URLs
RewriteCond %{REQUEST_FILENAME} !-f
RewriteCond %{REQUEST_FILENAME} !-d
RewriteRule ^(.*)$ index.php?q=$1 [L,QSA]

# Reduce server overhead by enabling output compression if supported.
#php_flag zlib.output_compression On
#php_value zlib.output_compression_level 5
```

If you are editing this file in Windows, make sure that the editor does not save any alien characters like ^M. It is preferable not to use WordPad, Word, Dreamweaver, or anything of that sort to edit the configuration files to avoid this happening.

Configure the **Friendly URLs** page in the Manager interface to meet your requirements. MODx makes it easier for you to configure the mapping of a URL to a friendly name pattern that you prefer.

The following is a screenshot of the configuration page for **Friendly URLs**. You can get to this page by clicking on **Configuration** on the **Tools** menu and then selecting the **Friendly URLs** tab.

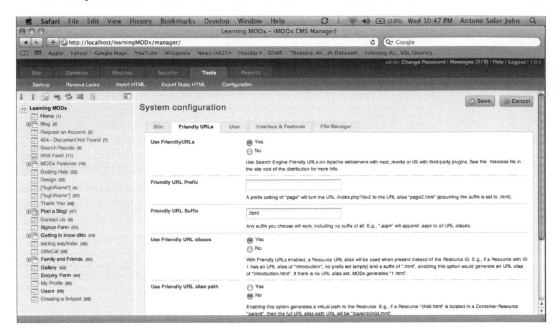

Change the **Use friendly URLs** option to **Yes**, and then click on **Save**.

Now you can go to the main page, `http://localhost/learningMODx`, and open any page using the menu. You will notice that the links have changed and are friendlier, now being in the form `http://localhost/learningMODx/pageid.html`.

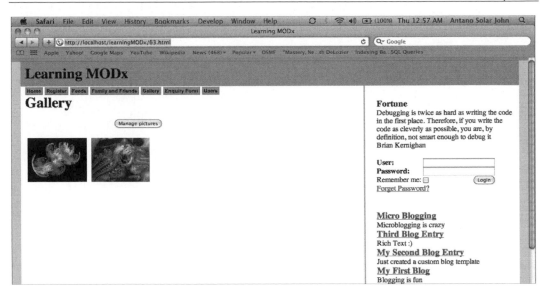

You can go ahead and change the prefix and suffix. By default, the prefix is blank and the suffix is `.html`, and that is the reason why you get `pageid.html`. I like to leave the `.html` prefix blank. This means you will have `http://localhost/learningMODx/pageid`.

The next option on the page is the **Use friendly aliases** option. When this option is turned on, the page can be accessed using the alias name instead of the ID. Our Home Page has the ID 1. Let us give it an alias. In the Friendly URLs configuration page, turn **Alias** to **On** and remove the `.html` suffix. Now try opening the URL `http://localhost/learningMODx/home`. You will see the Home Page. With the **Use alias** option, it is possible to access the resources by a name instead of a number.

The next option is the **Use friendly alias path**. This will make a resource accessible by its full path in the resource tree. Supposing the resource is a child of a container resource and both of these documents have aliases, then the document can be accessed by `http://localhost/learningMODx/parentalias/childalias`. Note that turning this option on would require you to turn the next option—**Allow duplicate aliases**—on, which is not recommended. Duplicate aliases mean that a resource can be accessed by more than one alias. This introduces an SEO problem. A site is more optimized for searching if every page has only one corresponding URL. That is, to access a particular page, there must be only one URL. This is known as *Canonicalization*. To make this happen, you can use the SEO Strict plugin, which will only allow the resource to be accessed by the exact alias. The next option is **Automatically generate alias**; turning this option on will automatically generate page aliases from the title of the page. Of course, you can still edit the generated aliases in case you want a different alias for a particular page.

Meta tags and keywords

Meta tags are a way for you to define what your website is about, to the outside world. These tags are generally placed within the `<head>` tag. Meta tags are specified by using the `<meta>` `</meta>` tags. These tags have two attributes—`name` and `content`. The `name` attribute is used to specify the name of the element, and the `content` attribute specifies the value for that element. For example:

```
<meta name="description" content="MODx reference">
```

There are a set of defined elements such as `author` and `description`. Setting these elements makes your site description clearer, and hence it will have a higher chance of getting a better rating. There is also an element called `keyword`, which can contain a list of space-separated words. The keyword element is used to inform the search engine about what content to expect on the site. Hence, setting the meta tags and keywords should make the site more search-engine optimized. With modern search engines however the meta tags and keywords really don't matter.

MODx used to come with a Manager interface that was used to add meta tags and keywords to the entire site. However, because it is easier to just add the meta tags and keyword in the templates or resources, this feature has been disabled in newer versions of MODx. However, if you want to enable this feature (which we don't recommended), you can do so from the **Configuration** menu item on the **Tools** menu (**Configuration** | **Tools** | **Show META Keywords** tab) in MODx.

To access this page once enabled, carry out the following steps:

1. Click on the **Elements** menu.
2. Click on the **Manage META** tags and **Keywords**.

You will see a screenshot like the example shown in the following screenshot:

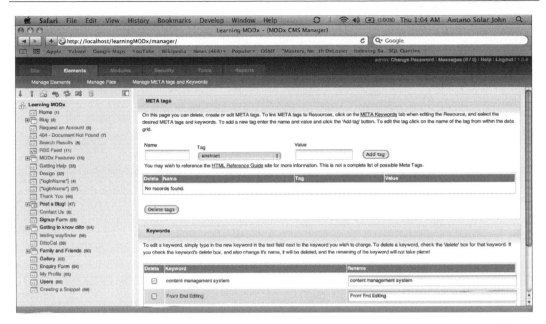

Here you can add, edit, and delete tags and keywords. This is rarely used, because the process for specifying keywords for an individual resource is rather cumbersome. Most people use a **Template Variable (TV)** to assign the keywords, and then, in their template, have the meta tag with the TV tag in place of a list of keywords. This way, you can easily edit the TV field for each resource.

Site map

A site map is an XML page that lets search engines know the layout of the site. Generally, you will have to create it yourself, but MODx has a snippet that does it for you automatically.

To use the snippet, perform the following steps:

1. Download the snippet from `http://modxcms.com/extras/package/?package=410`.

2. To install the snippet, click on **Create new snippet** in the **Elements Manager** and paste the code from the downloaded file.

3. Give the snippet the name `SiteMap`.

More instructions on installing snippets can be found in *Chapter 8, Snippets*.

4. Create a resource with the following details:

Field Name	Field Value
Title	SiteLayout
Uses template	(blank)
Content Type	text/xml
Resource content	[!SiteMap? &format=`sp`!]

Make sure that when you paste the preceding content, you are not using the rich text editor. This is a better practice when pasting code throughout the book. However, in this case, the code just won't work if you use a rich text editor.

5   Preview the SiteLayout page and you will see something like the following example in the source code, which contains a description of the entire site.

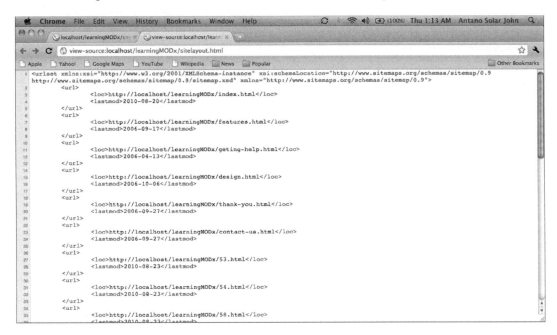

> **SiteMap Parameters**
>
> Google has a feature where you can check individual pages by using the site layout. You can do this by using the service provided by Google at http://www.google.com/webmasters/tools/.

XHTML Strict

It is good practice to use XHTML Strict conventions. This does make a difference in SEO. Unlike HTML, all XHTML tags have to be closed, and it is sometimes difficult to make a page XHTML-compliant when there is a lot of code mixed with it. Since MODx allows you to keep templates as plain XHTML with only variable replacements and snippet calls, it is easier in MODx to maintain XHTML strict compliance. You can always validate any page for complete compliance at `http://validator.w3.org/`.

Other SEO tweaks

In this section, we will quickly list a few other SEO tricks that aren't specific to MODx.

Using CSS to control the layout

Always use CSS to control the layout and don't mix it with the content. This also means that you should not use inline properties in HTML.

Content first

Always have the content as close to the `<body>` tag as possible. In the case of a site with large drop-down menus, have them placed in the bottom and use CSS to move them up.

Hidden text

Search engines, such as Google, consider hidden text to be misleading and remove such pages from indexing. Always make sure that you don't have text that machines can read but humans can't. An example would be a text box with size set to 1 pixel. When search engines encounter such pages, they tend to believe that you are trying to mislead the search.

Descriptive text

Always have descriptive texts for images, flash scripts, and any other objects that you embed. This not only helps people who use a screen reader to understand the contents of the site, but also helps the search engines.

Alternative text

It is a good practice to have alternate texts for all images used. What this means is that if the user for some reason can't see the image, the user at least gets to know what the image was for. Now search engines definitely can't see images!

Cross links

HTML and the web evolved because of cross-linking. Make sure that you link all pages in your site in as many relevant ways as possible. Search engines like a well-connected site.

Tracking

Use a tracking mechanism to monitor the changes in your site's hit ratio. Once you are aware of what works and what doesn't for your site, you will be able to tune it better. An example of such a tracking service is Google Analytics.

Inbound links

The more people that link to your site, the more likely it is that your site will appear at the top of the search results. Get more people to refer to your site. Somehow, this trend is picking up with the blogging community so rapidly that we are left with learning from them! Tools like Feedburner can help you track such stats for feeds. See `https://www.google.com/accounts/ServiceLogin?service=feedburner` for more information on Feedburner.

Quality content

Have quality content on your site. Quality content is not just what you have, it is also how you have structured it and placed it. With appropriate headings and relevant references, you are more likely to get a higher number of hits.

To know more, you may want to visit `http://www.google.com/support/webmasters/?hl=en`.

Deployment

Once you have completed the development of your website, you will want to make it available to the whole world. For this, you will have to deploy the website to a web server connected to the Internet. Any server that can run PHP and MySQL is suitable for MODx, and you can (at the time of writing) get an account starting from $3 a month. In this section, we will discuss what you need to move the website from one computer to another.

Filesystem

When migrating the website, you will have to copy the MODx installation root directory to the appropriate directory on your web server. There is not much that can go wrong in this process. Just make sure that all of the files are copied. Also, the transferred files may have different permissions on the new server. In such a case, the site will throw an error indicating the file permissions. If that happens, change the permissions accordingly, as described in *Chapter 2, Getting Started*.

Depending on your hosting provider, you will be given one of the ways described below of transferring files. There is an excellent full backup module that will zip up the whole filesystem and the database into a single ZIP file. You can then simply upload the ZIP file and unzip it by using the site control panel's *File Management* feature. The extracted folder will contain a file with the `.sql` extension. You can use this file to import the database by using phpMyAdmin, or any other database management interface that the hosting service provides.

FTP

FTP is one of the most commonly-used protocols for transferring files.

To get FTP on Windows, download the program called `winscp` from `http://winscp.net`.

Start the program, and specify the **User name** and **Password** that you have been given by your hosting provider. Enter the domain name and choose the **Protocol** as **FTP**.

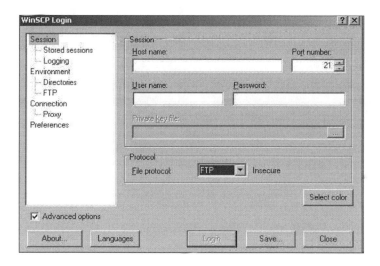

Click on **Connect**. You will see two panes—the left pane shows the files on your local machine, and the right side shows the files on the remote machine:

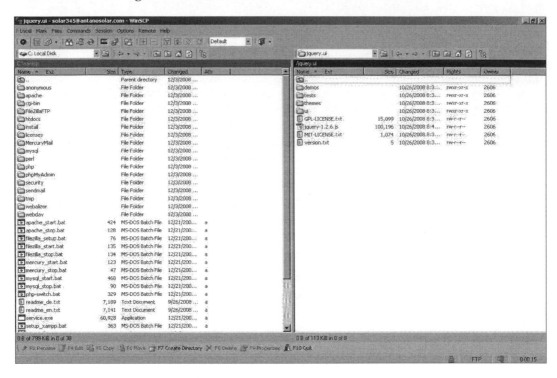

In Linux, you can use the `ftp` command to connect to the FTP server. Enter your username and password when prompted. (For example, `ftp antanosolar.com`.)

The `put` command helps you to transfer files from the local machine to the remote machine.

To transfer all of the files and folders within a folder, you can use the `-r` parameter. Just like regular filesystems, wild cards are accepted. `*` means all files, and `xyz*` means all files whose names start with `xyz`.

For example, `put * -r` will transfer all the files and folders, recursively.

The `get` command is used to transfer the files from the remote server to the local machine. It behaves in a similar way to `put`.

Alternatively, you can use a GUI-based client such as `kasablanca` or `kftpgrabber`. There is also another program called `curl`, which is worth trying. Curl can work over multiple protocols and is the preferred way by those who use Linux for their day-to-day activities.

SFTP

To install on Windows, follow the same steps as for FTP, but choose SFTP as the protocol, instead of FTP.

In Linux, there are two easy ways to transfer the files between the remote machine and the local machine using SFTP.

You can either familiarize yourself with the scp functionality—which is very similar to cp, which is used for copying files locally, or you can mount the remote filesystem locally and transfer files to and fro as you would do from a regular filesystem by using sshfs. It would be diverging from the topic to explain both scp and sshfs, but we will give you a few pointers here that can help you learn more.

scp is similar to cp. You have to specify two arguments—source and destination. If you want to copy a file named index.php from the current directory on the local machine to the remote machine, you would use the following command:

```
scp index.php username@remotemachineaddress:/foldername
```

Similarly, to transfer files from a remote machine to the local machine, you would use:

```
scp username@remotemachineaddress:/foldername localpath
```

sshfs is similar to mount. The only difference is that instead of mounting a local filesystem, you are mounting a remote filesystem. For this, you will need to first install sshfs. The general syntax is:

```
sshfs username@remotemachineaddress:/foldername /mountfoldername
```

You can alternatively use the application SecPanel, which has a GUI for scp.

WebDAV

WebDAV was originally meant for collaborative authoring, although these days it is also used for sharing files. WebDAV operates over the HTTP protocol. It is sometimes referred to as DAV, for short. To use a DAV resource, follow these steps:

In Windows:

1. Open **My Network Places**.
2. Click on **Add Network Place**.
3. Click on **Choose another network location**.
4. Enter the given URL from the service provider, followed by the username and password, in the Internet or network address box.
5. Now you will be able to access your files from **My Network Places**.

In Linux, the procedure to use a DAV resource is similar to mounting a filesystem over SFTP. You need to install an application called `fusedav` and then you can mount the filesystem locally. `fusedav` has the following syntax:

```
fusedav remoteurl /mountfoldername
```

Database

MODx stores all of the resources and templates that you create in the database. So you will have to transfer the database as well, in order for your site to be deployed. Almost all hosting providers provide phpMyAdmin for managing databases. There are two steps to migrating a database:

1. Export the database from the local machine.
2. Import the database to the remote machine.

Exporting

To export the database, you can use phpMyAdmin. We have already discussed the installation of phpMyAdmin in *Chapter 2, Getting Started*.

1. Log in to phpMyAdmin, using the MySQL username and password that you created for the database earlier, by opening the URL `http://localhost/phpmyadmin` in a browser.
2. You will see a list of the databases available on the server. Click on the database that you want to export.
3. Click on **Export**.
4. Select the **Save to file** checkbox, and click **Go**.

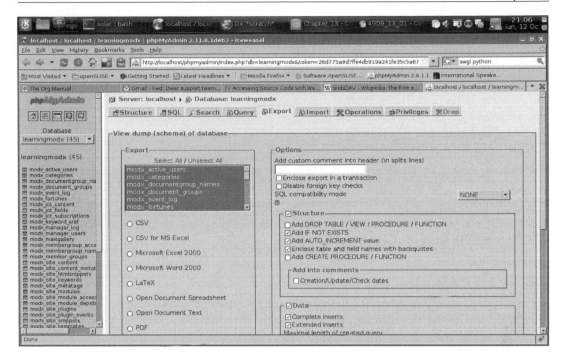

Importing

When you export a database, the default option is to save it as SQL, which means that the exported file contains the SQL instructions to reconstruct all of the tables and records in the database. Of course, you can choose a different formats and can even have them compressed before exporting. Once you have exported the database, you will want to import it to the remote server provided by your service provider.

1. Log in to phpMyAdmin by using the username **mySQL** and the password that was given to you by your service provider.

2. Create a new database, or select a database if you have already created one.

3. Click on **Import**.

4. Click **Browse** and select the file that was exported before.

5. Click on **Go** to import the database.

There is typically a server limitation on the size of the file that can be uploaded. The import screen shows the maximum size that can be uploaded. If the export file is larger than what your service provider allows you to import, try choosing a compression format to reduce the size. The compression works really well, and reduces the size of the exported file by a good ratio. Make sure that the compression format that you choose when exporting is also supported by the server onto which you are importing. When you click on **Import**, the screen shows the various compression formats that the server supports. **Bzip2** is known to offer the highest compression among the various compression formats that are supported.

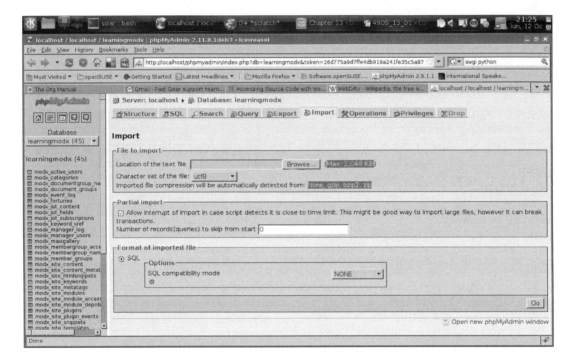

Configuration file

Sometimes you may not be able to use the same name for the database on the new server. Maybe the name is already taken. In such a case, it is alright to give a new database name, username, and password. You will have to make sure that you make the appropriate changes in the `manager/includes/config.inc.php` file and upload it back to the server.

```
<?php
/**
 *      MODx Configuration file
 */
$database_type = 'mysql';
$database_server = 'localhost';
$database_user = 'root';
$database_password = '';
$database_connection_charset = '';
$dbase = '`learningmodx`';
$table_prefix = 'modx_';
error_reporting(E_ALL & ~E_NOTICE);

$lastInstallTime = 1211112170;

$site_sessionname = 'SN48301aea4d284';
$https_port = '443';

// automatically assign base_path and base_url
if(empty($base_path)||empty($base_url)||$_REQUEST['base_path']||$_REQUEST['base_url']) {
    $sapi= 'undefined';
    if (!strstr($_SERVER['PHP_SELF'], $_SERVER['SCRIPT_NAME']) && ($sapi= @ php_sapi_name()) == 'cgi') {
        $script_name= $_SERVER['PHP_SELF'];
    } else {
        $script_name= $_SERVER['SCRIPT_NAME'];
    }
    $a= explode("/manager", str_replace("\\", "/", dirname($script_name)));
    if (count($a) > 1)
        array_pop($a);
    $url= implode("manager", $a);
    reset($a);
```

Configurations

Depending on the path of the new location, you might also want to change the following settings in the Manager, by clicking on the **Tools** menu and selecting **Configuration**.

- **File base** path in **Interface & Features**
- **File Manager** path in **File Manager**

[If you had created other Managers' accounts, it may also be necessary to edit these fields for them, individually.]

Security

In this section, we will discuss the permissions on filesystems that have to be set in order to make sure that your site is safe. Also, we will discuss captcha and the mod_security module for Apache, which can cause certain issues arising from security concerns and how to solve them. When using a content management server, unless you are writing snippets yourself, there is not much to worry about. There are a few things to keep in mind though, for MODx, and they are mentioned next.

File permissions

It is a good practice to set read-only permissions on all files except folders that will be updated by MODx. In Linux, you can do this through chmod 0644 * -R within the MODx directory. Some folders must be made writable by using chmod 0755 folder. The following is a list of such folders:

- assets/cache
- assets/files
- assets/media

When you are using an external snippet that requires you to store files in a separate folder, make sure that you make those files writable too. For example, the gallery snippet we saw earlier requires that the folder assets/galleries be writable. For more details on what chmod does, please refer to *Chapter 2, Getting Started*.

Installer

The MODx installer files are stored in the install directory. Make sure that you delete this folder after installation. Leaving it on the system poses a security risk, and someone may try to install MODx on your system again.

Writable configuration file

MODx stores the configuration of the site in manager/includes/config.inc. php. This file contains the database connection details and other settings. However, during installation, this file has to be made writable, as MODx will have to store the settings that you enter in the web page. After the installation is complete, you must make it read-only, in order to have a secured site.

Captcha

Captcha is a technology to prevent spam bots. There are malicious machines on the Internet that have programs that can automatically register and post to blogs, and so on. Such programs are called **bots**. Captcha shows an image containing embedded text and asks the user to enter the same in a textbox. This makes sure that the person filling the form, or registering, is a human and not an automated machine. Most MODx snippets that accept input from the user have captcha ability. Make sure that you use captcha wherever necessary, in order to make your site spam free.

mod_security

Apache has a security module that checks for code in POST requests and blocks it, which means, that if you are adding a snippet using the Manager and submit the form, then there are chances that the code may be considered unsafe. In such a case, the snippet will not get saved. In such situations, you can disable the security module for the duration of the post. On a hosted server, this may not be possible. Instead, what you can do on hosted servers is to write a few additions to the .htaccess file that will permit the data transfer.

You can try one of the following two lines in the .htaccess file:

- To turn off post data filtering:

  ```
  SecFilterScanPOST Off
  ```

- To turn off the security filter engine:

  ```
  SecFilterEngine Off
  ```

 For any changes in .htaccess to take effect, the Apache server has to be restarted.

Unused files

A recent security exploit demonstrated that unused .php files should never be left in the filesystem. They should either be deleted or renamed (such as the .php files that are included with snippets, plugins, and so on that contain the code to be copied into the Manager). This experience will also most likely teach the snippet authors to name their Manager code files with a different suffix as well, even if this does prevent an editor's syntax coloring (by default) from working properly on the file.

Manager configurations

In addition to the previously-mentioned security issues, there are simple configurations in the Manager that can help you to make your site even more secure. These options can be found when clicking on **Configurations** on the **Tools** menu.

User tab

The following are the options that the **User** tab supports:

- **Failed Login Attempts**: This option specifies how many times to allow a user to enter a wrong username or password consecutively, before the user is blocked. This can be useful to prevent a brute force attack, where a program, or even a person, is trying to guess the password of another user.

- **Blocked Minutes**: This option specifies how many minutes to block the user for before allowing them to attempt to log in again.

File Manager tab

New File Permissions: Here you can set the default permissions for the files that are being uploaded. 0644 is safe, and it is the default permission. This makes sure that the files are not writable, but are executable by everyone.

New Folder Permissions: Here you can set the default permissions for the new folders that you create by using the File Manager. The default permission — 0755 — again, is a very safe option.

Uploadable File Types: In this textbox, you can specify a list of comma-separated file extensions that can be uploaded to the site. It is important that you specify non-executable extensions. It is a good idea to only allow extensions that you are anticipating; for example, if you want to allow the uploading of images, only then you can give the list of .gif, .jpeg, and .tif.

Summary

In this chapter, we discussed how to make the site optimized for search engines. We discussed clean URLs, meta tags, site maps, and other tweaks. Having developed the site on a local machine, we learned in this chapter how to deploy it to a remote server. Finally, we looked into what has to be done in order to make your MODx site secure.

13
Plugins and Modules

This chapter explains plugins and modules, including those that we have used in our application. This chapter also covers events and plugin configuration.

Plugins and events

Plugins are PHP code blocks in MODx that, unlike snippets, are not called for execution from a resource or a template. Rather, plugins are executed on the triggering of certain events, when a resource is parsed, or during other internal processing. Every action in MODx, such as rendering a resource, or deleting a user from the system, will trigger a series of flags. Each flag is viewed as an event. For example, you have events such as:

- `OnDocFormPrerender` — triggered just before the resource is going to be rendered
- `OnUserFormSave` — triggered just before the user's details are saved

There are many such events, and we will not describe each one of them in this chapter. Rather, we will discuss how to write plugins that are executed in response to specific events. We will also describe how to generate events—even custom ones—when you are writing snippets.

We will start by first examining some plugins that should have been installed during the setup, and gradually move into creating a very basic plugin.

Using an existing plugin

You can view the entire available plugins list by clicking on **Elements | Manage Elements | Plugins**. An example of such a plugin list is shown below:

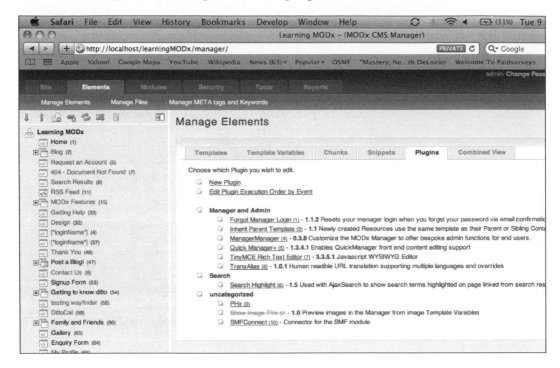

You will notice that **PHx**—which we used earlier—is also a plugin. Click on the PHx plugin to explore it further.

As you can see from the next screenshot, a plugin is similar to a snippet, in that it has a plugin name and some PHP code.

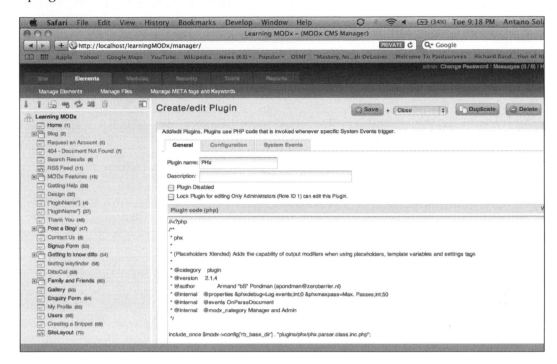

You will also see two other tabs, namely **Configuration** and **System Events**. Let us look into each of these tabs.

Configuration

The configuration screen (as shown in the next screenshot) has category selection boxes for the plugin just like any other element in MODx. There is also an option called **Import module shared properties**, which we will discuss in the next section, on modules.

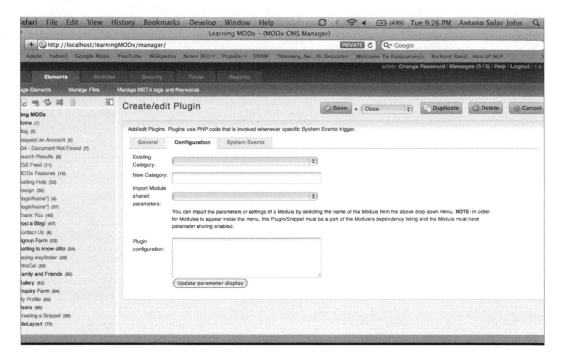

Using the Plugin Configuration text area, you can pass parameters to the plugin. There is a specific syntax to do so. All values have to be passed as a `key : value` pair, with pairs separated by commas. There are five parts to a configuration parameter—the parameter name, its label, the data type, optional values, and a default value. Each parameter must begin with &. The parameter values are separated by a semicolon.

The following example is taken from the **TinyMCE** plugin:

```
&entity_encoding=Entity Encoding;list;named,numeric,raw;raw
```

This defines a configuration variable named `entity_encoding`. The label used when displaying the parameter editing form will be **Entity Encoding**. Its type is a `list`, with three options—`named`, `numeric`, and `raw`. The default value is `raw`.

System events

In this screen, you will see a list of events.

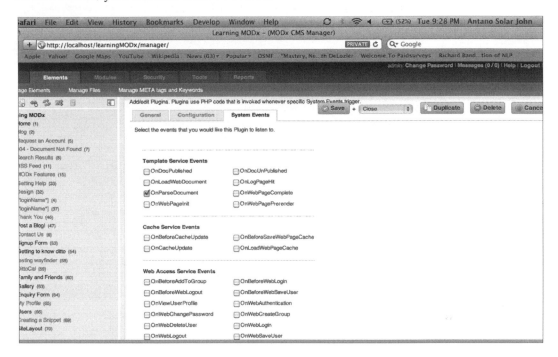

When the checkbox next to any event is selected, the plugin will be executed when that event happens. For example, we are viewing the PHx plugin and, as we can see, the checkbox next to **onParseDocument** is selected. This will make MODx execute the PHP code for the PHx snippet just before parsing the document.

If you take a moment now to think about how PHx works, you will understand the whole concept better. MODx fetches a resource and, just before parsing, executes the PHx plugin. The code in the PHx plugin is written to search and replace the PHx notations with their corresponding result. In the subsection on creating plugins, we will discuss how to take a resource, process it, and send it back to MODx as output.

 All Events still refer to Resources as Documents, as in the earlier versions of MODx.

Exploring other plugins

Now is a good time to go through the other plugins and notice their triggering events. It will help your understanding to think about why the **Quick Manager+** plugin is triggered by the **OnWebPagePrerender** event, and so on with other plugins.

Using custom plugins

In this section, we will download a plugin called Codeprettify and learn how to use it. The following steps describe how to do this:

1. Download the plugin from http://modxcms.com/extras/ package/?package=75, and then extract it.

2. Click on **New plugin** from **Elements** | **Manage Elements** | **Plugins**.

3. Fill in the following details:

Field Name	Field Value
Plugin name	Code Prettify
Plugin code	Copy and paste the code from plugin.codeprettify.tpl
Configuration ->Existing Category	Learning Modx
System Events	OnLoadWebDocument: Checked

4. Click on **Save.**

5. Copy the codeprettify directory that you have extracted, to the assets/plugins directory.

 Note that it doesn't matter what name you give the plugin, as you will not be invoking it by any call; rather it gets invoked on execution of the selected events automatically.

As stated, for all elements, a category is just used to allow the developer to visually group the elements, and doesn't affect the functionality.

If you notice the selected **System Events**, the trigger is **OnLoadWebDocument**. You may wonder why it is not **OnWebPagePrerender**. This is because this plugin inserts JavaScript, and it is better to do so before the resource is even generated.

Now let's go ahead and test the plugin.

Create a resource with the following details:

Field Name	Field Value
Title	Testing Plugin
Uses Template	Learning Modx default template
Document content	echo "This code is pretty printed by the new plugin";

Now, a preview of the resource will look like the example shown in the following screenshot:

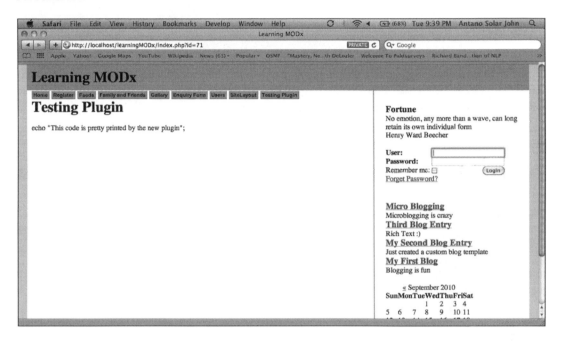

As you can see, there is no visible difference; this is because this plugin requires all of the code that has to be prettified to be inserted within:

```
<pre class="prettyprint"> </pre>
```

So, to test pretty printing, change the contents of the resource to the following:

```
<pre class="prettyprint">
echo "This code is pretty printed by the new plugin";
</pre>
```

Now the preview will look like the example shown in the following screenshot:

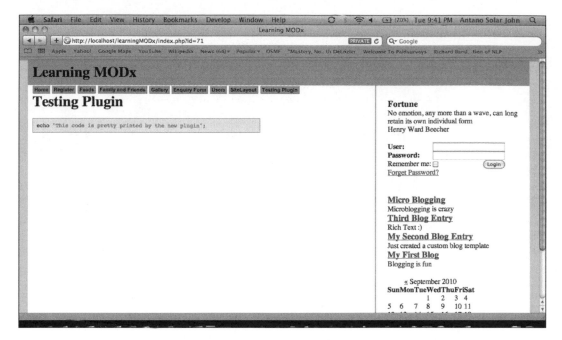

Learning about the plugin

When using the previous plugin, there were a few details that we couldn't have intuitively known. For instance, we couldn't have known which tags are to be used in the resource and which events have to be enabled. Therefore, it is important that for every plugin that you want to use you read the associated document. Many plugins come with a separate document; some have the details on the download page. However, some plugins have usage details commented in the file that contains the plugin code. In our previous example, we got the details from the plugin code.

As you can see if you open the `plugin.codeprettify.tpl` file, the top section contains the following code:

```
/*
 * CodePrettify *
 *
 * DESCRIPTION: Allows syntax highlighting of code blocks, using the
 * google-code-prettify javascript
 *
 * HISTORY:
 * version 0.5 (2007-09-08): by Daniele "MadMage" Calisi
 *
```

```
 * NOTES: google-code-prettify can be downloaded from Google Code
website (http://code.google.com/p/google-code-prettify/)
 * and is under the Apache 2.0 license
      (http://www.apache.org/licenses)
 *
 * INSTRUCTIONS:
 * - extract the content of the zip archive in
                 assets/plugins/codeprettify
 * - create a new MODx plugin using the code of this file
 * - select "OnLoadWebDocument" as the System Event that will trigger
                                               this plugin
 * - all source code in the webpage enclosed in <code
                 class="prettyprint">...</code>
 *   or in <pre class="prettyprint">...</pre> will be automatically
                                               prettified.
 * - you can optionally put some css in assets/plugins/codeprettify/
prettify-custom.css file
 */
```

One key skill that is very important in leveraging a community-driven platform like MODx is to be able to search and read through documentation. This may, in many cases, help you to avoid having to reinvent the wheel, and help you to find quicker solution for something that is challenging your mental abilities. As an old friend once said—"IT Consultants get paid for reading documents".

Creating plugins

To create a plugin, you just have to remember this one concept: the plugin code requires a wrapper to determine what to execute in which event.

MODx passes the event details to the plugin along with the MODx elements, which we examined in *Chapter 12, PHx*. $MODx->Event holds the details of the event. $MODx->Event->name gives you the name of the event. So, the plugin code will have to check the name of the triggered event and execute the appropriate code. This can easily be done with a switch statement. Hence, the structure of code specific to the events in a plugin would look like this:

```
$e = & $MODx->Event;
switch ($e->name) {
  case "eventname1" :
                  Code for eventname1
                  break;
  case "eventname2" :
                  Code for eventname2
                  break;
```

```
default              :
                return;
                break;
```

Now is a good time to look into the source code of the previous plugin. By doing so you will be able to understand exactly how the plugin works the way it does. If you want to use external files in your plugin, then the convention is to place these files in a separate folder within the assets/plugins directory. The following is the code from the plugin that we just used:

```
switch ($MODx->Event->name) {
  case "OnLoadWebDocument":
      $MODx->regClientCSS('assets/plugins/
            codeprettify/prettify.css');
      $MODx->regClientCSS('assets/plugins/codeprettify/prettify-
                                            custom.css');
      $MODx->regClientStartupScript('manager/media/script/mootools/
                                            mootools.js');
      $MODx->regClientStartupScript('assets/plugins/codeprettify/
                                            prettify.js');
      $jspp = '<script type="text/javascript">';
      $jspp .= 'window.addEvent("domready", prettyPrint);';
      $jspp .= '</script>';
      $MODx->regClientStartupScript($jspp);
      break;
  default:  // stop here
      return;
      break;
}
```

Similar to what you have just learned, the plugin uses a switch case to check for the event, along with the $MODx->Event->name API. We can see that it executes a portion of the code for only the OnLoadWebDocument event, and for any other event, it just returns without changing anything.

Let us now examine what the previous code does. The code uses an API that we haven't yet discussed. The following table explains the APIs.

Field Name	Field Value
$MODx->regClientCSS	This API can be used to load a CSS at the beginning of the page. The CSS loaded by using this function will be inserted within the <head></head> tag. The function takes one argument, which is the name of the CSS file, or the CSS content itself.
regClientStartupScript	This API is similar to the previous API, but in this case, it loads a JavaScript file within the <head></head> tag, instead of the CSS.

As you can see, the discussed plugin does the following two things:

1. Inserts the <style .... /> tag for CSS
2. Inserts the <script ...></script> tag for JavaScript

This plugin, as described in the comments, is using a JavaScript function from Google Code that already does the pretty printing. The functionality of this plugin is to just ensure that the JavaScript code and the CSS are loaded for every resource, irrespective of the template used. As you may realize, plugins affect the system-wide behavior for the selected events.

Event-triggering snippets

It is possible to trigger events from your snippets, in order to get a plugin to do something.

The API to do this is $MODx->invokeEvent. invokeEvent takes two parameters, namely the name of the event and the parameters to be passed. For example:

```
$MODx->invokeEvent("OnBeforeWebLogin", $parameters);
```

> It is recommended that you do not use this API, as it is intended to be used by the core code. If you are curious anyway, and want to try it, going through the code of WebloginPE will help.

Modules

In this section, we will learn how to use modules, and see how a module works.

Modules are code that can be executed only from the Manager interface. Modules are useful for the following two purposes:

1. Adding functionality to the `Manager` interface.

    An example of this kind of functionality is the **DOC Manager** module, which is an optional component that can be installed during the MODx installation. This module allows the Manager to perform bulk actions on resources.

2. Creating tables that snippets can use.

    Snippets and plugins may need to store data in the database. Modules can facilitate this by creating these tables for the snippets or plugins. Moreover, Modules can be used to create an interface for the Manager to add data. This data can be stored in the database for snippets or plugins to use. In this section, we will look into a module and plugin pair, in order to demonstrate this functionality.

Using modules

In this section, we will install a module called **Autolink**. This module provides the Manager with an interface that can be used to create the keywords that the accompanying snippet can use. The following are the steps to use the module:

Creating a module

1. Download the module and the plugin package from `http://modxcms.com/extras/package/?package=30`, and then extract it.
2. Click on **New Module** from **Modules | Manage Modules**.
3. Fill in the following details:

Field Name	Field Value
Module name	Autolink
Module code	Code from `autolink_module.txt`
Category	`Learning MODx`

4. Click on **Save**.

Executing a module

Once you have created a module, you will have to manually execute it from the `Manager` interface. The following steps show you how to do this:

1. You will see the module listed along with the other modules.
2. Next to the module, there is a small icon. Clicking on this icon opens a context menu.

3. Click on **Run Module** in the **Context** menu.

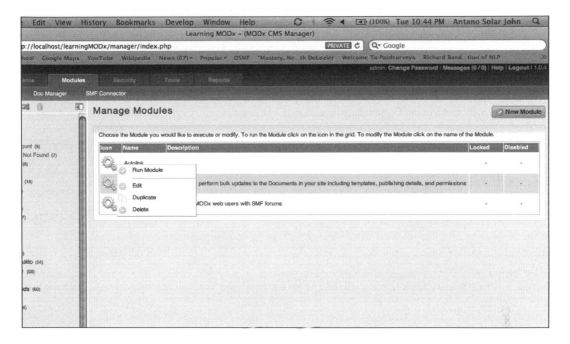

Module's Manager interface

Running the **Autolink** module provides us with a page that allows us to define the keywords that will be used by the plugin. The plugin replaces the keywords with a pre-defined link. Let us, for now, just add one keyword—**MODx**—with the value **google**. This should allow the plugin to create a link that searches for "MODx" in Google.

1. Click on **Add Keywords** in **Modules | Manage Modules | Autolink**.
2. Fill in the following details:

Field Name	Field Value
Keyword	MODx
Value	google
Title	Google MODx

3. Click on **Add Keywords** at the bottom of the form.

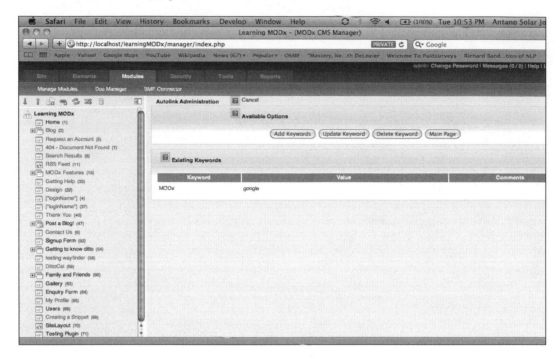

Dependent plugins

Now that we have installed the module that allows the creation of keywords from the Manager interface, let us create and install the accompanying plugin that will convert the keywords to links in a resource.

1. Click on **New plugin** from **Elements | Manage Elements | Plugins**.
2. Fill in the following data:

Field Name	Field Value
Plugin name	Autolink
Plugin code	Code from autolink_plugin_v2.txt
Configuration	Category	Learning MODx
System Events	OnWebPagePrerender: checked

3. Click on **Save**.

Let us test the combined functionality of the module and its plugin by creating a resource with the following contents:

Field Name	Field Value
Title	Testing Modules
Uses template	`Learning MODx` default template
Resource content	`<autolink>`
	`MODx`
	`</autolink>`

Now preview the preceding document, and it will look like the one shown in the following screenshot:

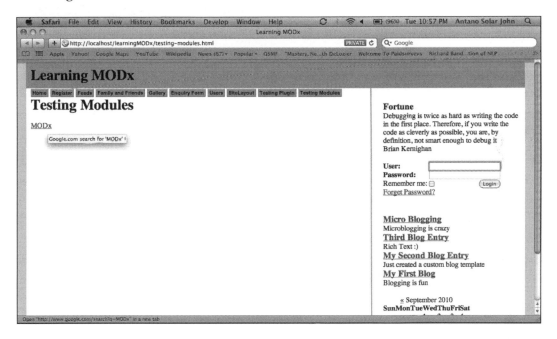

You may notice that the keyword has been changed to a link that is a Google search for "MODx". This is shown in the status bar at the bottom of the browser window, and the title is used for the tooltip. The plugin retrieved these values from what we inserted into the Modules page.

Remember that this section is teaching you how to use modules and not Autolink. You must also remember that there is no need to have a relationship between the module name and the plugin name. The plugin merely reads the values from the database by using the regular MODx db API that we discussed earlier.

```
Ex: $rs = $MODx->db->select('*', $autolinkTable);
```

Unlike snippets and plugins, we will not learn how to create modules, as efficient use of modules may require our understanding of certain design patterns.

Learning to use custom modules

Because the installation of modules and plugins involves multiple steps, it can be a little confusing in the beginning. It will be very easy to understand if you keep in mind a few points. Modules are used for providing some functionality in the Manager interface, and for sharing the results of such interaction, such as data collected, with plugins and snippets.

Summary

In this chapter, we have learned about plugins and modules.

- The differences between plugins and modules are:
    - Snippets are executed when they are explicitly called either in a resource, a template, or from another snippet.
    - Plugins are executed on the trigger of the events with which they are associated. This allows the plugin code to be executed just before resource rendering, user registration, and so on, as needed.
    - Modules are executed only from within the Manager. They are used for creating the tables that dependent plugins or snippets may want to use. Modules can also provide an interface in order to give values to the plugin and snippet parameters.
- You have learned how to use plugins and how to customize plugins.
- You have also learned how to create new plugins, and we analyzed the code of the prettify code plugin that we used.
- Finally, you have learned how to use modules by using the Autolink module and plugin, and saw an example of this.

14
MODx Revolution

Congratulations! You have done very well. You are now equipped with the tools and techniques that are required to rapidly build high-quality websites with MODx. In this chapter, we will catch up with some upcoming features that will make your development experience even better. This chapter introduces the MODx Revolution, so that when it is there, you are not left behind.

Why Evolution, why Revolution...

You may wonder why you want to stick with Evolution when Revolution is already available for download. Evolution has been around for many years now and is very stable, with lots of plugins and snippets that work out of the box. It has been well tested, and many professional websites are already using MODx Evolution. Revolution, on the other hand, has only a release candidate this year, and the snippets and plugins available in Evolution may not work.

Also, the major reason for using Evolution is this: you can migrate from Evolution to Revolution at any time. So you can wait until a stable release is available and then make the migration. Nevertheless, it is good to be prepared, and armed with the knowledge of what is ahead. In this chapter, we will discover just that.

What is similar?

The methodology remains the same, be it Evolution or Revolution. The core of everything is a resource. A resource can use a template and make snippet calls. Plugins still get executed on specific events. What really has changed is the very core on which MODx is built, which allows for quicker development of many features, and removes certain restrictions.

What to expect?

As explained in the preceding section, what has really changed is the core, which allows for quicker and easier development of new features. The following is a list of the many features that are already available as an effect of the core changes. This information is edited from the official MODx roadmap, which can be found at: `http://modxcms.com/develop/roadmap.html`.

- New manager: The new manager has been redesigned to be more friendly and customizable. The manager is on its way to become fully-customizable through templates.

- Packages: Now elements can be installed, updated, and maintained from the MODx manager interface.
  In the future, Revolution will also allow installation from remote repositories.

- Contexts: Imagine being able to reuse and share your elements in different contexts. Also, think of the contexts having a hierarchy! MODx Revolution introduces contexts, which make it easier to manage subdomains, subsites, multisites, and so on.

 For more information on contexts, please read: `http://rtfm.modx.com/display/revolution20/Contexts`.

- Improved security: With some of the core changes, like no `eval`, Revolution definitely paves the way for some serious security improvements.

- Improved caching: Caching has been improved in the core, database, and partial pages. This will improve the performance of your site by a large degree and is a major development in the right direction.

- Improved content parser: Now content parsing is possible without using many regular expressions! And you can nest `[[ tags]]` to any level.

  As Jamie Zawinski quoted:

  "Some people, when confronted with a problem, think "I know, I'll use regular expressions." Now they have two problems."

Tags

For those who are in a hurry to migrate, you may find the following information useful. MODx Revolution now uses a unified tag format. The following table shows an official listing of the changes in the tag format. In a nutshell, now every tag is in the [[ ]] format. This table is taken from the official documentation at http://modxcms.com/develop/roadmap.html .

Element	Old Format	New Format
Template Variables	[*templatevar*]	[[*templatevar]]
Chunks	{{chunk}}	[[$chunk]]
Snippets	[[snippet]]	[[snippet]]
Placeholders	[+placeholder+]	[[+placeholder]]
Links	[~link~]	[[~link]]
System Settings	[(system_setting)]	[[++system_setting]]

A peek into Revolution

The preceding sections provided you with a peek into the screens of MODx Revolution. Feel free to install MODx Revolution and try it yourself.

Revolution Login Screen

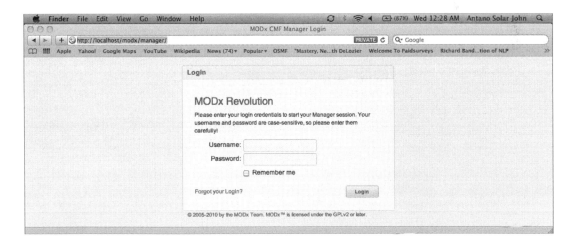

Manager Home

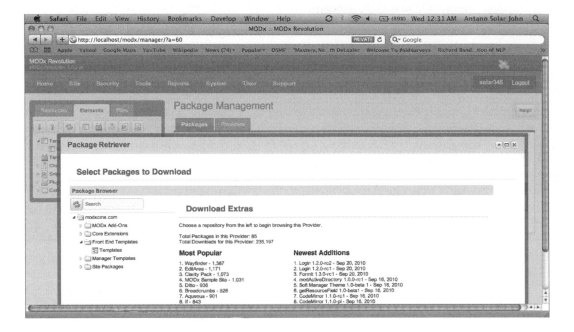

Installing Extras from within the Manager

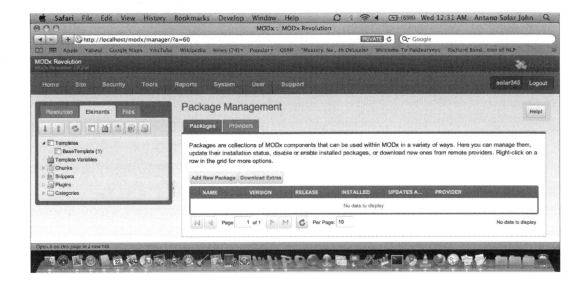

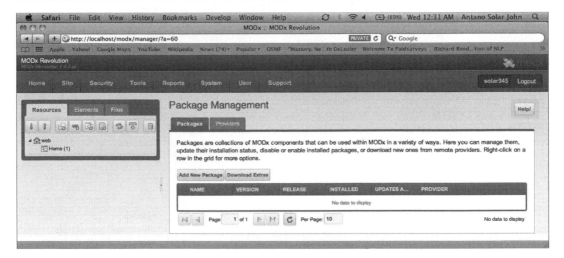

Inline Help

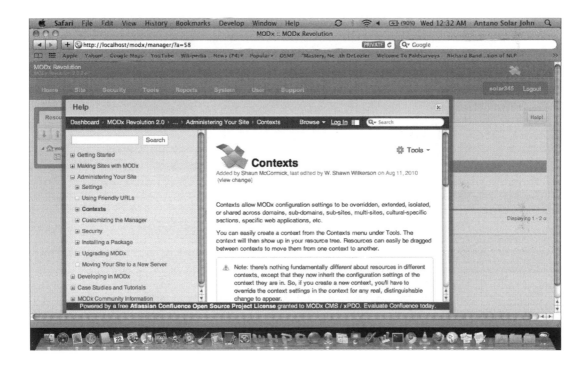

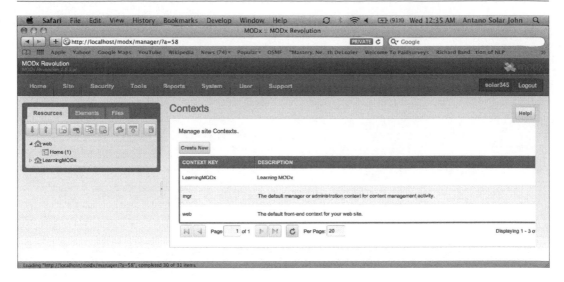

Contexts

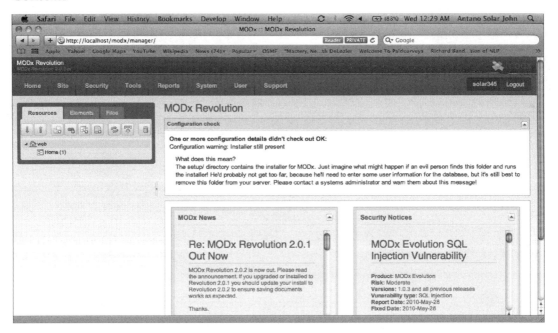

MVC using actions from within Manager

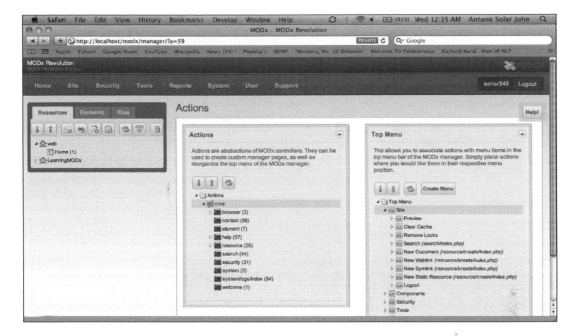

Lexicon Management

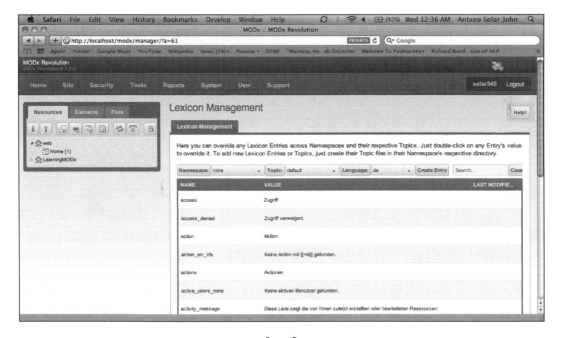

Core technology changes

Finally, a section for PHP developers and all of those who are curious to know more about the core technology changes in MODx Revolution:

xPDO

MODx has a completely new object-oriented core, rewritten using xPDO. xPDO is an Object Relational Bridge. This is a concept where SQL tables are mapped as objects in the system. This means that they can be manipulated as objects. This is very convenient in an object-oriented environment. Although MVC frameworks have popularized ORB concepts, you don't always need an MVC to make use of xPDO. This also means that, if you are a developer extending MODx at the core or by writing new snippets, you will also benefit from the ease and simplicity of this approach. The new object-oriented approach also provides you with an improved API. This in turn makes the core extendable with content parsing, session handling, and so on.

Sencha and Smarty

MODx Revolution makes use of the Smarty framework for delivering the frontend manager. This means that it is easier to theme the manager interface. MODx revolution also uses Sencha, which makes it easier for developers to create drag-and-drop functionalities and other AJAX features. This also means less testing for cross-browser compatibility and so on.

Join the community

If you are fascinated by all of the developments going around in MODx, join the community today at `http://modxcms.com/community/forums.html` and start shaping the future of MODx.

Summary

In this chapter, we have taken a quick look into MODx Revolution, to understand when to upgrade, what to expect, and how to contribute. I hope you had fun with the Revolution from Evolution.

Index

N

name
  changing, of site 38
name attribute 220
nested menus 121, 122
new plugin
  creating, MODx Manager interface used
    160
New Resource icon 41
NewsEditor 65, 69, 70, 78
NewsPublisher 98
new template
  creating 53
new template, creating
  about 53
  CSS code 54
  HTML code 53
New Weblink icon 41
non-bundled snippets
  using 151
non-cached call 138

O

Object-Relational Mapping. *See* **ORM**
official documentation 32
OnDocFormPrerender event 235
OnUserFormSave event 235
ORM 13
or operator 112
output
  generating, spinnets used 69

P

pages
  removing, from menu 131
parameters
  using 205, 206
parents parameter 100
PHP 10, 19
phpMyAdmin
  about 209, 225
  database, exporting with 228
PHx
  about 159, 236
  conditional statements 171

  downloading 160
  Family and Friends page, creating 160, 161
  functionality, adding to site 159
  installing 160
  modifiers 170
  multiple conditions 172, 173
  template variable, formatting 170
  URL, for downloading 160
PHx placeholder
  using 171
PHx wiki documentation
  URL 173
pidgin 34
placeholders
  about 57, 99, 103, 148, 149
  returning 203
Place Holders extended. *See* **PHx**
plugin.codeprettify.tpl file 242
plugins
  about 235
  creating 243, 244
Post a Blog! page
  custom form, using for 71
  verifying 74, 75
post moderation
  about 92
  Manager user, creating 93, 94
  role, creating 92
  role, verifying 94
Purge icon 41
put command 226

Q

quality content 224

R

rand() function 210
rating 61
readers 107, 108
Really Simple Syndication. *See* **RSS**
Refresh Site Tree icon 41
regClientStartupScript field 245
register_globals 38
resource group 90

Thank you for buying
MODx 2.0 Web Development

About Packt Publishing

Packt, pronounced 'packed', published its first book "*Mastering phpMyAdmin for Effective MySQL Management*" in April 2004 and subsequently continued to specialize in publishing highly focused books on specific technologies and solutions.

Our books and publications share the experiences of your fellow IT professionals in adapting and customizing today's systems, applications, and frameworks. Our solution based books give you the knowledge and power to customize the software and technologies you're using to get the job done. Packt books are more specific and less general than the IT books you have seen in the past. Our unique business model allows us to bring you more focused information, giving you more of what you need to know, and less of what you don't.

Packt is a modern, yet unique publishing company, which focuses on producing quality, cutting-edge books for communities of developers, administrators, and newbies alike. For more information, please visit our website: www.packtpub.com.

About Packt Open Source

In 2010, Packt launched two new brands, Packt Open Source and Packt Enterprise, in order to continue its focus on specialization. This book is part of the Packt Open Source brand, home to books published on software built around Open Source licences, and offering information to anybody from advanced developers to budding web designers. The Open Source brand also runs Packt's Open Source Royalty Scheme, by which Packt gives a royalty to each Open Source project about whose software a book is sold.

Writing for Packt

We welcome all inquiries from people who are interested in authoring. Book proposals should be sent to author@packtpub.com. If your book idea is still at an early stage and you would like to discuss it first before writing a formal book proposal, contact us; one of our commissioning editors will get in touch with you.

We're not just looking for published authors; if you have strong technical skills but no writing experience, our experienced editors can help you develop a writing career, or simply get some additional reward for your expertise.

CMS Design Using PHP and jQuery

ISBN: 978-1-84951-252-7   Paperback: 340 pages

Build robust and reliable persistence solutions for your enterprise Java application

1. Create a completely functional and a professional looking CMS

2. Add a modular architecture to your CMS and create template-driven web designs

3. Use jQuery plugins to enhance the "feel" of your CMS

PHP 5 CMS Framework Development - 2nd Edition

ISBN: 978-1-84951-134-6   Paperback: 416 pages

This book takes you through the creation of a working architecture for a PHP 5-based framework for web applications, stepping you through the design and major implementation issues, right through to explanations of working code examples

1. Learn about the design choices involved in the creation of advanced web oriented PHP systems

2. Build an infrastructure for web applications that provides high functionality while avoiding pre-empting styling choices

3. Implement solid mechanisms for common features such as menus, presentation services, user management, and more

Please check **www.PacktPub.com** for information on our titles

CMS Made Simple 1.6: Beginner's Guide

ISBN: 978-1-847198-20-4   Paperback: 364 pages

Create a fully functional and professional website using CMS Made Simple

1. Learn everything there is to know about setting up a professional website in CMS Made Simple

2. Implement your own design into CMS Made Simple with the help of the easy-to-use template engine

3. Create photo galleries with LightBox and implement many other JQuery effects like interactive navigation in your website

Kentico CMS 5 Website Development: Beginner's Guide

ISBN: 978-1-84969-058-4   Paperback: 312 pages

A clear, hands-on guide to build websites that get the most out of Kentico CMS 5's many powerful features

1. Create websites that meet real-life requirements using example sites built with easy-to-follow steps

2. Learn from easy-to-use examples to build a dynamic website

3. Learn best practices to make your site more discoverable

Please check **www.PacktPub.com** for information on our titles

Printed in Great Britain by
Amazon.co.uk, Ltd.,
Marston Gate.

1529773R0